T0333034

MARVEL STUDIOS

100 OBJECTS

ICONIC ARTIFACTS FROM THE MCU

MARVEL STUDIOS
100 OBJECTS

ICONIC ARTIFACTS FROM THE MCU

TRACEY MILLER-ZARNEKE

Contents

MYSTICAL MIGHT

ESSENTIAL EQUIPMENT

BATTLE READY

SUPERIOR SCIENCE

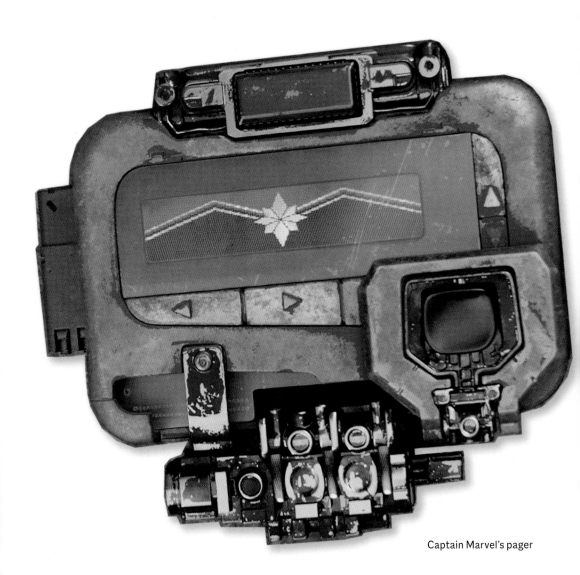

Captain Marvel's pager

Author's Note

The Marvel Cinematic Universe is infinitely rich with imagination... spanning time, space, reality, and every other continuum touched by the Infinity Stones, thanks to creative forces as talented as there are stars in the galaxy. This imagination has touched generations of audiences at such a profound level that young fans aspire to be as brave as Captain Marvel, as innovative as Shuri, as bold as Tony Stark, or as charming as Peter Quill; all ages of viewers find adventure and enthrallment visiting the planets from Asgard to Xandar and everywhere in between; and many wish they could have the freedom to hop timelines and shape-shift as deftly as Loki.

It is with homage to this sense of intergalactic fascination that I welcome you to tour the 100 objects presented in this book. Without any intention of equating myself to an omniscient Cosmic Being, please know that for the authorial standpoint, I have adopted the position of an "all-seeing eye," in order to recount the stories of the selected items.

From ancient artifacts dating back to the distant past, to ingenious devices that feel futuristic, these objects reflect something of the creative expanse of the MCU. These historical, scientific, technological, and mystical wonders serve as landmarks on the journey through stories we have all enjoyed for decades, as well as time spent with characters we have all come to know and love.

I hope you explore this collection with the warmth of nostalgia and a depth of connection to the incredible legacy of the MCU, and carry it forward with you to anywhere else your imagination may take you beyond this curated tour.

Tracey Miller-Zarneke

Artifacts
of Interest

Over the course of Marvel Cinematic
Universe history, a number of important
items have stood the test of time and
relevance, and each one has an intriguing
story to tell. From ancient tomes and
cassette tapes, and from ceremonial
masks to a secret society medallion, the
following collection of objects represents
some of the key cultures, individuals, and
organizations that have helped to shape
the MCU.

1

Asgard Fresco

Seen by: Residents and visitors to Asgard's royal palace
Years in use: The distant past to 2017

Spectacular decorations chronicling events in the life of Odin and his family once graced the walls and ceilings of the halls of Asgard's royal palace. However, the representations of *which* moments in history were worthy of depiction varied dramatically over time.

These earlier images reflected the conquests that King Odin and Hela wrought upon surrounding realms—ambitious and bloodthirsty war tours, rife with cruelty and plunder—in order to establish the wealth and power of Asgard. But as Odin developed a more conciliatory approach to kingship, he banished his warmongering daughter and sought to rewrite Asgardian history, striking references to Hela and their joint conquests from all records and revamping the fresco storytelling. Updated, overlaid images depicted peaceful views of Odin with his queen Frigga and their royal family (from which Hela was omitted), comprising their son Thor, and their adopted son, Loki.

The existence of layers of frescoes in the palace was revealed after Hela was released from banishment following her father Odin's death. During her revenge-laden return to Asgard and attempt to reclaim what she regarded as her rightful place on the throne, she angrily toured the palace halls and struck at the palace walls with her swords. The tranquil, regal images of Odin's rule crumbled away, uncovering Asgard's long-hidden, warlike past, and Hela's significant part in it.

These original frescoes remained in place until the utter destruction of Asgard came to pass during the fiery manifestation of Ragnarok.

2

The Book of Yggdrasil

Used by: Odin, the Asgardian people, Johann Schmidt
Years in use: The distant past to 2017

An ancient Asgardian tome, *The Book of Yggdrasil* contained an illustrated, magical, detailed history of the Nine Realms. Yggdrasil was portrayed as a figurative tree that supported and connected the Nine Realms of the universe.

Although its exact point of origin is unknown, the original book was last housed in Asgard. The royal family of Asgard turned to *The Book of Yggdrasil* to inspire younger generations. Queen Frigga often regaled her children Thor and Loki with the book's heroic stories of the past.

The Book of Yggdrasil also chronicled knowledge beyond storybook-style entertainment. It told the tale of the Dark Elves through time. It foretold the Convergence of the Nine Realms as an occurrence due to happen every 5,000 years, opening space/time passageways between realms beyond the single Bifrost conduit through space that was managed by Asgard.

One of the book's most remarkable features was the enchantment contained within its pages that enabled its stories to animate in their telling; for example, depicting scenes of the Dark Elves building their mystical Aether weapon to help them fight the light once it began to shine in the Nine Realms.

Odin drew upon the wisdom he had learned from its pages when faced with the resurgence of the Dark Elves. Unfortunately, the tome had no help to offer Jane Foster when she asked how the Dark Elves' insidious Aether weapon might be separated from its unwilling host—herself.

A less magical copy of *The Book of Yggdrasil* came into the possession of Hydra during World War II. This copy was found in a church in Tønsberg, Norway, and included a history of Odin and his family. Interestingly, and perhaps not coincidentally, Tønsberg was the location in which Odin won one of his fiercest battles, against King Laufey of the Frost Giants, birth father of Odin's adopted son, Loki. However, the most intriguing information found in this edition of the book—at least from the perspective of Hydra leader Johann Schmidt, alias the Red Skull—concerned the Tesseract. This artifact, which housed the Space Stone, had become an

Om Konung Sigurds resa til
Constantinopel.

obsession for Schmidt, who sought to use its energy to craft weaponry formidable enough to dominate the globe.

A counterfeit Tesseract was hidden in the coffin of a dead Viking warrior to distract thieves, but Schmidt soon discovered the true one. He noticed an ancient carving in the church that depicted the "World Tree" Yggdrasil. Divining a link with the book of the same name, he found a secret drawer containing the Tesseract. Upon this discovery, Schmidt ultimately confirmed the Space Stone's vast powers, as described in *The Book of Yggdrasil.*

While the original Asgardian book is presumed to have been destroyed during Ragnarok in 2017, the whereabouts of this second edition remain unknown in the present day.

The story of Odin's father Bor's defeat of the Dark Elves of Swartalfheim is one of the many important Asgardian legends of the Nine Realms contained in the book.

This page from the book illustrates the overlapping portals of the Convergence.

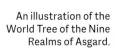

An illustration of the World Tree of the Nine Realms of Asgard.

3

The Throne of Asgard

Used by: Asgardian royalty

Years in use: The distant past to 2017

For centuries upon centuries, multiple generations of Odin's family sought to rule the Nine Realms from this magnificent throne.

Odin inherited the throne and authority over the Nine Realms from his father Bor, best known for his valiant battles against Malekith, leader of the Dark Elves during the Convergence of the Nine Realms. Bor successfully prevented the Dark Elves from employing the mystical powers of the Aether, which would have plunged the universe into total darkness. Upon Bor's death in battle, his son became the king of Asgard.

In more recent times, Odin's death left a power vacuum in Asgard. Odin's firstborn, daughter Hela—whose bloodthirsty tendencies had caused Odin to banish her from the kingdom—sought the throne. Odin's adopted son, Loki, also had an obsessive desire to take his place as king, even shape-shifting to impersonate Odin to achieve this goal. Odin's own son, Thor, who had the right and opportunity to inherit the throne, eventually declined, deciding that he would "rather be a good man than a great king." This decision, influenced by his romantic relationship with Jane Foster, briefly enabled Loki to take power.

The golden throne presented its honored ruler seated atop a grand, golden staircase. Similar flights of steps on either side of the throne allowed the king to approach his throne from the side if he so desired. The king took his seat in front of an ornate, double-columned panel, and between the carvings of two raven guardians.

The throne shone in all its glory for centuries, but is presumed to have been destroyed in 2017 by Surtur during Ragnarok, the long-prophesied destruction of Asgard.

4

Captain America's Sketchbook

Used by: Steve Rogers
Years in use: The 1940s

This sketchbook contains drawings by Steve Rogers, dating back to World War II. Although he became known for his heroic efforts as Captain America, judging from the images in the book, he could have had a successful career as a commercial artist.

These circus-like drawings were drawn by Rogers during several difficult early public appearances as the US's one and only super soldier, Captain America—"the Star-Spangled Man with a plan"—accompanied by a female dance troupe. They suggest Rogers' deep dissatisfaction with his allotted wartime role. Colonel Chester Phillips, his commanding officer in the Strategic Scientific Reserve (SSR), only uses him as a vacuous performer, boosting the profile of the U.S. military and driving up sales of war bonds. Rogers longs to fight in genuine warzones alongside his peers, which include his best friend James Buchanan "Bucky" Barnes, a sergeant in the 107th Infantry.

Encouraged and helped by the SSR's Agent Carter, Rogers soon becomes far more than the dancing monkey and costumed clown he channels in his artwork. Agent Carter welcomes him into the SSR's operation to defeat the Hydra organization, and later Cap participates fully in the work of the Strategic Homeland Intervention, Enforcement and Logistics Division (S.H.I.E.L.D.).

From then on, Steve Rogers dedicates himself to the role of the first Avenger, Captain America. His drawing of the dancing monkey—a reminder of his previous struggles—stands near his desk while he watches news of the United Nations' Sokovia Accords conference in Vienna, an event that will spark discord among the Avengers.

5

S.H.I.E.L.D. Insignia

Use: Displayed on S.H.I.E.L.D. locations, uniforms, and equipment
Years in use: 1946 to 2014

This symbol is the insignia of the Strategic Homeland Intervention, Enforcement and Logistics Division better known by the acronym S.H.I.E.L.D. Founded in 1946, this U.S. governmental organization was established as a counter-terrorism and intelligence agency meant to support both national and global security. Its predecessor organization during World War II was known as the Strategic Scientific Reserve (SSR), and a key figure in that group, Agent Carter, became the first director of S.H.I.E.L.D., invited to take on the position by Colonel Chester Phillips and inventor Howard Stark, with whom she had served in the SSR.

S.H.I.E.L.D. is credited with a number of notable accomplishments in the fields of science and global security. For example, the early scientific work of Howard Stark, Hank Pym, and Bill Foster paved the way for innovative security operations involving vibranium, particle manipulation, and quantum energy.

These achievements are later manifested through the work of the Avengers Initiative, a team of uniquely-abled individuals who come to include Iron Man, Black Widow, Captain America, Hawkeye, Thor, and the Hulk, among others, as assembled by S.H.I.E.L.D. director Nick Fury in the early 2000s.

S.H.I.E.L.D. also co-opts the work of former World War II foe and Hydra researcher Arnim Zola to exploit his scientific expertise. The agency later comes to regret this, as Zola proves responsible for infiltrating S.H.I.E.L.D. with Hydra agents. The internal corruption of S.H.I.E.L.D. by Hydra comes to a head in 2014 when Director Nick Fury is attacked while investigating a supposedly anti-terrorist program named Project Insight and shot by Hydra agent the Winter Soldier. In the wake of that attack, Fury chooses to fake his death to work under the radar, put a stop to Project Insight—saving 20 million innocent lives—and expose Hydra's infiltration of S.H.I.E.L.D.

The insignia for S.H.I.E.L.D. has evolved over the decades of the agency's existence, but always features the graphic of an eagle.

6

Throne of The Ten Rings

Used by: Wenwu, Shang-Chi, Xialing

Years in use: Unknown to the present day

The Ten Rings refers to both a physical grouping of ten mystical rings as well as a criminal organization, so named because of its founder Wenwu's use of The Ten Rings. Although their origins are unknown, The Ten Rings are hewn from a metal-like material, the nature of which has yet to be determined, even after evaluation by a range of experts including Dr. Bruce Banner, Captain Carol Danvers, and Sorcerer Supreme Wong. The Ten Rings can emit powerful energy blasts and serve as effective weapons as projectile items that rebound to the person who possesses them. They also provide the user with the ability to levitate and to fly.

Another powerful effect bestowed by The Ten Rings is longevity. The Ten Rings are known to have existed among the possessions of the warlord Wenwu for thousands of years. With these ten metallic rings adorning his arms, Wenwu embarked on conquest after conquest around the world for centuries, training warriors to fight alongside him in a paramilitary organization also known as The Ten Rings. The throne of The Ten Rings was his official seat of power.

Wenwu's obsession with conquest continues until he extends his mission into another realm, searching for the legendary city of Ta Lo. Access to Ta Lo can only be achieved via a mystical bamboo-forest-protected portal in China, which only reveals itself once a year.

Upon finally arriving in Ta Lo in 1996, Wenwu encounters one of its human protectors, Ying Li. He falls in love with her and decides to set aside his life of conquest. The couple live a quiet life raising a family of four together in China until Wenwu's past comes back to haunt him. A foe in the Iron Gang comes seeking retribution and takes Li's life. The family is devastated, and Wenwu decides to take up the power of The Ten Rings again and to direct his 14-year-old son Shang-Chi to avenge his mother's death. While the revenge sought is a success, this act of violence revolts Shang-Chi and alienates him from his father's renewed ambitions of

A metal relief of The Ten Rings adorns the wall behind the throne.

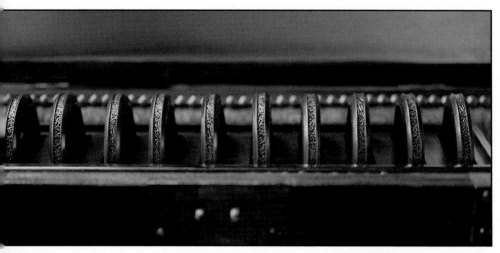

The Ten Rings are stored instead of worn while Wenwu tries to live a peaceful life with his young family.

conquest. They go their separate ways, and Shang-Chi hopes to live a simple life of peace in San Francisco.

Wenwu's revitalized Ten Rings empowerment continues to spread havoc around the world. The warriors of his organization use terrorist tactics and employ firepower from the latest weapons developed by Stark Industries. A Ten Rings cell is hired to eliminate Tony Stark by Obadiah Stane—formerly his father Howard's business partner.

The experience of being injured by Stark weapons himself and witnessing the massive global damage they can cause makes Tony realize how easily Stark Industries' inventions can be used for evil purposes. He resolves to change the purpose and direction of Stark Industries, and help to counter this potential evil through his own invention, Iron Man, a persona and suit of armor crafted when he and Dr. Ho Yinsen were imprisoned by a Ten Rings cell.

In 2024, after a family reunion does not go according to Wenwu's plan of jointly reentering Ta Lo, Shang-Chi comes to possess The Ten Rings and the immortality enjoyed by Wenwu comes to an end. Xialing, Shang-Chi's sister, becomes the head of The Ten Rings organization.

he revamped throne room,
s reimagined by the new leader
f The Ten Rings, Xialing.

7

Dark Elves' Mask

Used by: The Dark Elves

Years in use: The distant past to 2013

Masks such as this, with pale skin, pointed ears, large forehead, and deep-set eyes, were worn by some of the oldest inhabitants of the universe, the Dark Elves of Svartalfheim. Their home realm was in a quadrant of the universe that was overwhelmed by dark matter. Its single source of natural light came from the dwindling energy of a dying star.

As *The Book of Yggdrasil* recounted, the Dark Elves existed unchallenged as "shadow-dwellers" before stars began to emit light and warmth, which eventually created other forms of life in the universe. The Dark Elves battled the existence of light as it was counter to their well-being; in fact, they created a powerful weapon known as the Aether that turned matter into dark matter to support this effort.

The Asgardians, led by King Bor, tore the Aether from the Dark Elves' grasp in battle during the Convergence of 2988 BCE. Malekith, the Dark Elves' leader, sacrificed his own people in a futile attempt to destroy the Asgardian army, but without the Aether, Malekith was defeated. Unable to destroy the Aether, Bor instructed his men to bury it where it would never be found.

The Asgardians believed that Malekith and the Dark Elves were no more; however, they were simply in hibernation. The inadvertent rediscovery of the Aether by Jane Foster awakened them, and the approach of another Convergence of the Nine Realms in 2013 gave Malekith and his masked elvish army the chance to reclaim their world of darkness, destroy Asgard, and remake the universe to their liking.

During the Convergence, Malekith and his army were defeated by Thor and his human comrades in a ferocious battle in Greenwich, London.

8

Loki's Helmet

Used by: Loki

Years in use: The ancient past to 2017

This impressive helmet was one of several worn by Prince Loki of Asgard during his adult life. The golden metal of its construction and the sweep of its horns served to dramatically advertise Loki's royal status. Whenever Loki donned this helmet he was an undeniably intimidating sight. Loki became part of the royal family in the year 965 when Odin took pity upon the abandoned biological son of the Frost Giant King Laufey. Odin raised him as his own son alongside his son Thor.

Loki wore this helmet with supreme pride and confidence on many occasions, such as when he attempted to destroy Jotunheim and wipe out the Frost Giants to prove to Odin that he was worthy to succeed him as king. The last public occasion when he donned it was during the Chitauri Invasion of 2012, specifically in the Battle of New York. During this clash, Loki turned against his adoptive brother Thor and was defeated and captured in combat against the Hulk. During the fight he lost possession of this helmet.

In 2017, Loki embarked upon an endeavor to defend Asgard during which he was seen wearing a smaller version of the golden-horned helm. In this battle, Loki realigned with Thor and together they fought against their sister Hela's violent rampage. Loki seemingly lost his helmet battling soldiers belonging to her undead army. Although this effort to defeat Hela was successful, the horned helmet was not recovered, presumably because it—along with all other objects and life-forms in Asgard—was destroyed following the apocalyptic onset of Ragnarok.

9

The Red Hydra Codebook

Used by: Hydra and other nefarious organizations and individuals
Years in use: The late 1940s to 2018

The Winter Soldier is a scientifically modified human assassin developed by Hydra during the 1940s and 1950s. Between missions, he was preserved in cryogenic stasis.

The Red Hydra Codebook contained essential information regarding the programming of this almost unstoppable killing unit. For decades, Hydra employed the Winter Soldier to incite political crises and wars around the world. The Winter Soldier also undertook assassination missions, such as the 1991 murder of Howard Stark and his wife Maria to facilitate Hydra's acquisition of Stark's Super Soldier Serum, and an attempt to eliminate S.H.I.E.L.D. director Nick Fury.

The most valuable information in the codebook was the string of phrases that triggered the activation of the Winter Soldier program in James Buchanan Barnes. Captain America's World War II comrade "Bucky" Barnes was believed killed in action. In reality, Barnes had been captured, brainwashed, and with a cybernetic limb replacing his missing left arm, become the prototype for Hydra's Winter Soldier Program. A spoken sequence of Russian words, listed in the codebook, initiated the Winter Soldier's assassination protocol. The English translation was: Longing, Rusted, Furnace, Daybreak, Seventeen, Benign, Nine, Homecoming, One, Freight Car.

Throughout its existence, the codebook was stolen time and again by scientists, government agents, and double agents wishing to exploit the Winter Soldier's power. The information it contained began to lose its power over Bucky once Captain America realized that the Winter Soldier and his former childhood and army buddy were one and the same. The deprogramming of the Winter Soldier was accomplished by the Wakandan scientist Shuri in 2018. Bucky recovered his humanity, and the book no longer had any control over him.

The codebook contains a wealth of information about the Winter Soldier's past missions.

10

Awesome Mix Vol. 2

Used by: Star-Lord
Years in use: 1988 to 2014

This cassette was given to a young Peter Quill, alias Star-Lord, by his mother, Meredith Quill. She recorded her favorite songs onto two blank cassettes, Awesome Mix Vol. 1 and Vol. 2, specially for him. The songs on the tapes form an essential soundtrack to Peter's life as a space-faring vagabond.

Peter equips his spacecraft, the *Milano*, with a console that plays his beloved tapes. He values his portable cassette player so highly that he fights a prison guard to get it back during his risky escape from the Kyln intergalactic penitentiary. Peter later tries to romance warrior and assassin Gamora with a carefully chosen track. The music on his cassette tapes is also an effective diversionary tactic to confuse particularly grim opponents, such as Ronan the Accuser, with whom Quill and the Guardians of the Galaxy have a close encounter on the planet Xandar. Quill isn't the only music lover among the Guardians: Baby Groot also enjoys a dance to Quill's tape while the others are fighting a monster.

Awesome Mix Vols. 1 and 2 are among Quill's most prized possessions, until Quill's father, the Celestial Ego, smashes the portable player (containing Vol. 2) in a fit of fury when his son refuses to agree with his plans to expand his being throughout the universe. The event is doubly traumatic for Quill as he has just learned that his father caused his mother's death by giving her the brain tumor that cut short her life.

Quill later replaces the cassette player with a portable digital music player with 300 songs on it.

11

Prosthetic Leg

Used by: A Kyln inmate, Star-Lord
Year in use: 2014

This prosthetic human limb is purchased from a prisoner in the Kyln, an intergalactic penitentiary, by Star-Lord Peter Quill as part of an escape plan developed by fellow inmate Rocket. The Kyln is run by the Nova Corps, the military/police force of the Nova Empire, which has apprehended Rocket, Quill, Gamora, and Groot after a street fight over bounty rights and the Orb.

Once incarcerated, these four inmates decide to join forces and escape. Rocket, the brains behind the breakout, says he requires three things in a specific order: a security band from a prison guard, a prosthetic leg, and, lastly, a quarnyx battery, in order to access the Kyln's watchtower. Unfortunately Groot gets hold of the battery first, activating the prison's emergency system, chaos ensues, and the group has to fight its way out. At one point Quill uses the leg as a handy club to knock out a prison guard. Rocket later reveals that the inclusion of the leg on the list of items was just a joke. The humor is lost on Quill, who has paid a prisoner 30,000 units for it. The group reach the watchtower and Rocket uses the quarnyx battery to disable the Kyln's artificial gravity, causing all the guards and inmates to float harmlessly in the air. The success of the jailbreak is a big win for the motley crew of Quill, Rocket, Gamora, Groot, and a new associate, Drax the Destroyer. The group subsequently adopt the name the Guardians of the Galaxy, a moniker sarcastically given them by their enemy, Kree extremist Ronan the Accuser.

Collecting artificial human body parts turns out to be something of a hobby for Rocket. In addition to this prosthetic item, Rocket subsequently offers to share his possession of an artificial human eye with Thor, and tries to convince Bucky Barnes, alias the Winter Soldier, to sell him his high-tech, weaponized, artificial arm.

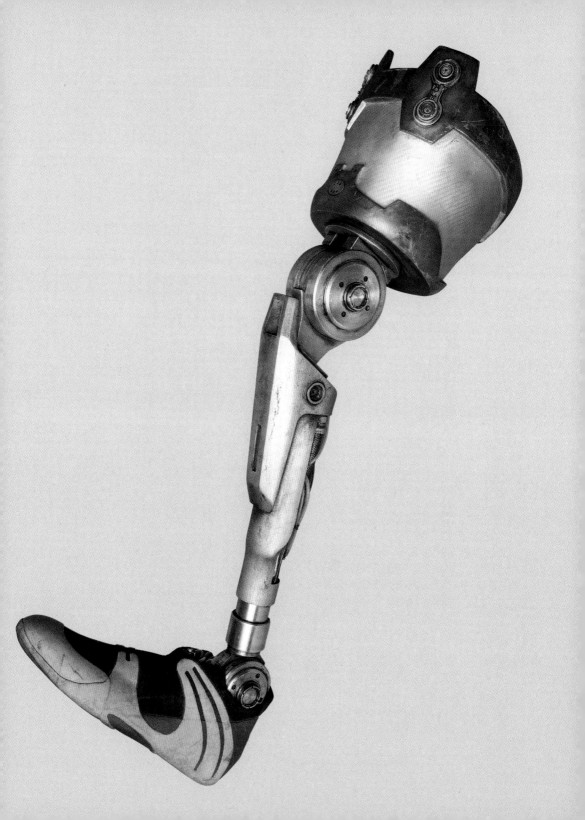

12

The Sokovia Accords

Used by: The United Nations, S.H.I.E.L.D., the Avengers
Years in use: 2016 to 2025

In the wake of the death and massive destruction wrought when the battle against Ultron exploded within the Eastern European country of Sokovia, governments all over the world feel compelled to draft an agreement governing the work of agencies such as S.H.I.E.L.D., and specifically the superpowered abilities of the Avengers and other enhanced individuals. Described as a "Framework for the Registration and Deployment of Enhanced Individuals," the Sokovia Accords are designed to regulate superpowered activities. They are drawn up by the United Nations Security Council and ratified by 117 countries.

The Sokovia Accords trigger worldwide controversy about their effect on basic human rights and civil liberties. In particular, the new regulations stir up discord among the Avengers themselves, who are well aware of public disquiet over whether they are protectors of the greater good or vigilantes with the power of mass destruction.

Following further collateral damage in Lagos, U.S. Secretary of State Thaddeus Ross seeks to persuade the Avengers to support the Accords. The Avengers split into two camps. After experiencing deep remorse over the loss of innocent lives battling the threat of Ultron, Tony Stark (Iron Man) supports the Accords. However Steve Rogers (Captain America) strongly resists, unwilling for the Avengers to be controlled by the UN. The two Avengers factions engage in unresolved battle at Leipzig-Halle Airport.

The success of Thanos' Snap and the removal from existence of half the planet's population stands as the most dramatic case study of the dangers of disunity among the Avengers' ranks. The Sokovia Accords remain in effect for nearly a decade before they are repealed in 2025.

Graffitti in Sokovia underlines public dissatisfaction with the Avengers.

THE
SOKOVIA ACCORDS

FRAMEWORK FOR THE REGISTRATION
AND
DEPLOYMENT
OF
ENHANCED INDIVIDUALS

Registered by the United Kingdom of Great Britain, Austria, Germany, Russia
Italy, France, Northern Ireland, and the United States of America

13

Doctor Strange's Watch

Worn by: Doctor Strange
Years in use: 2016 to the present day

This timepiece is a gift to surgeon Dr. Stephen Strange from Dr. Christine Palmer, a medical colleague and, at the time, his girlfriend. The watch is a luxury model, the back of which is inscribed: "Time will tell how much I love you. Christine."

The watch is a precious possession for Dr. Strange, who wears it on special occasions. One night he is driving to a black-tie event, only to be involved in a devastating car accident in which he loses the use of his hands. The watch is broken in this traumatic incident, but Strange continues to wear it, even after the end of his relationship with Christine. This precious link to his past life is the only personal possession he takes to the mystical retreat of Kamar-Taj on his journey to becoming Doctor Strange, a Master of the Mystic Arts.

Later, when Doctor Strange enters an alternate version of Earth with the Multiversal traveler America Chavez, he witnesses Christine presenting an alternate version of himself with a brand-new version of the watch during a romantic dinner for two.

Following the death of that world's Doctor Strange, the watch—damaged now—passes into Christine's possession. When Doctor Strange, Christine, and America are menaced by The Scarlet Witch, the watch proves to be the key to opening the Gap Junction, where Doctor Strange finds the *Book of Vishanti*, a vital tool in combating The Scarlet Witch's *Darkhold* magic.

The watch may be said to symbolize the importance of time and time-travel in Doctor Strange's world. This is exemplified by his development of skills that allow him to traverse the Multiverse and by his eventual defeat of Dormammu, ruler of the Dark Dimension, accomplished by his use of the Time Stone in trapping this opponent in a time loop.

It is only after his victory over Dormammu, and when Doctor Strange accepts that Christine has moved on and married someone else, that the watch is finally repaired by Doctor Strange and put away—for now.

14

The Royal Ring of Wakanda

Used by: T'Chaka, T'Challa

Years in use: Unknown to the present day

This piece of jewelry is an important heirloom of Wakandan royalty. The metal ring—its composition is unknown—was previously worn by T'Challa, who had taken ownership of it following his father T'Chaka's death in a bomb explosion at a United Nations conference in Sokovia in 2016.

T'Challa wore the ring for the duration of his time serving as the King of Wakanda. It is presumed that the ring was handed down in this way from generation to generation of Wakandan rulers. This lineage may be traced back to the establishment of a collective of four tribes that had been warring among themselves prior to the warrior Bashenga's shamanic unifying presence. A fifth tribe, the Jabari, chose not to join, preferring to isolate itself in Wakanda's mountainous regions. Bashenga subsequently became the first Black Panther and also king of Wakanda.

The royal ring with its oval, shield-like motif represents the natural strength and power of the Wakandan people, as carried throughout history by its royal rulers. The desire for control of the kingdom with its invaluable vibranium resources causes great instability to Wakanda, attracting various power-hungry persons. These include N'Jadaka, alias Erik "Killmonger" Stevens, who believes that he—and not his cousin T'Challa—should be the rightful king and wear the royal ring.

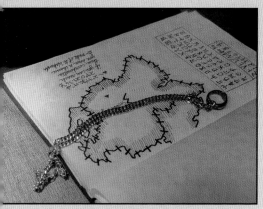

N'Jadaka's father N'Jobu leaves him vital objects to equip him to rule, including a book showing a map of Wakanda and his own ring on a golden chain.

15

Traditional African Mask

Used by: Erik "Killmonger" Stevens
Years in use: Unknown to 2016

Although the exact age of this African mask is unknown, what is known is that it was officially displayed in the Museum of Great Britain until it was stolen by Erik "Killmonger" Stevens in 2016. This sinister-looking artifact was a particularly appropriate choice of attire for the ruthless Killmonger. He wore it when he broke Ulysses Klaue, his partner in an illegal vibranium trade, out of a safehouse in the city of Busan, South Korea, interrupting his interrogation by C.I.A. agent Everett Ross.

Killmonger's interest in vibranium had deep familial links, as his father, N'Jobu, was smuggling vibranium from Wakanda to spark worldwide revolution in partnership with Klaue when Killmonger was a boy. This illegal trade ceased when N'Jobu's efforts were revealed to his elder brother T'Chaka, the King of Wakanda, who, in the heat of confrontation, killed N'Jobu. Young orphan Erik was inspired to follow his father's example and use Wakanda's valuable vibranium resources to create weapons to fuel a global uprising of the world's oppressed people.

Killmonger grew up in Oakland, California, and trained as a U.S. Navy Seal. He eventually earned the nickname "Killmonger" because of his success in eliminating human targets through his work in the black-ops unit. These skills empowered him to pursue his goal of high-risk, high-stakes vibranium dealings, and drove him to depose his cousin T'Challa—whom he despised as the "son of a murderer"—as King of Wakanda for a short while. During a second face-off with his cousin, Killmonger received a mortal wound and, refusing medical aid, chose to die with honor.

16

The Throne of Wakanda

Used by: T'Chaka, T'Challa, N'Jadaka, Queen Ramonda, and earlier generations of rulers
Years in use: Unknown to the present day

This regal seat is the royal throne of the kingdom of Wakanda, a small country in Africa. Wakanda is perhaps the most technologically advanced country on Earth but has kept its true vibrancy hidden from the greater world for centuries to conceal its rich resource of vibranium, an extremely rare metal embedded in the region by way of a meteor collision with the planet millions of years ago. Only in more recent times has Wakanda allowed itself a thoughtful and guarded entry into the grander scale of interaction within the world at large.

The design of the throne exudes majesty—creating a powerful setting for Wakanda's sovereign. It is crafted with an elegant black finish that is reflective of the Black Panther, a presence that holds great cultural value in Wakanda. According to legend, the panther goddess Bast decided that a Black Panther protector would always keep watch over Wakanda; Bashenga was the first human to embody that role. The role of Black Panther has passed from generation to generation, often but not consistently overlapping with the individual named King of Wakanda. The throne is flanked by black panther statues, a strong sculptural portrayal of this powerful relationship.

In modern times, the nation's focus on innovation is notably channeled into the work of the Wakandan Design Group, which supports the entire kingdom by utilizing the country's wealth of vibranium in its application of advanced scientific and technological skills to create vital tools, weaponry, communication means, transportation modes, as well as a cutting-edge wardrobe for the Black Panther protector.

The political power of the throne itself draws interest and conflict at times, with challengers for it coming into play as part of Wakandan tradition. In the wake of the death of T'Chaka, M'Baku of the neighboring Jabari Tribe challenges T'Challa, the son of T'Chaka, for its honor but does

not succeed in that moment. Later, T'Challa is challenged by his cousin N'Jadaka, alias Erik Killmonger—whose victory leads to greater conflict within the kingdom.

The importance of the Black Panther as an icon in Wakandan culture is symbolically clear in a number of ways. The grandest homage is most impressively displayed as a sculpture that looms on a mountainside overlooking the bustling capital city, depicting a powerfully protective presence. Courtesy of technologically masterful Wakandan security, this gigantic Black Panther remains invisible beneath a holographic projection of jungle areas, open plains, and forested hills that shield it—and the true advanced technology of Wakanda—from detection by observation from above, including satellite and radar-based surveillance.

This much smaller but still menacing version of the protective Black Panther is one of a pair flanking the throne room.

The imposing royal throne room of
Wakanda—before it was destroyed by
Namor's invading Talokanil army.

Although this method of camouflage proves effective, it remains
susceptible to infiltration from below. On the one-year anniversary of
T'Challa's passing in 2025, Namor of the Talokanil tribe approaches
Wakanda from the depths of the sea. During this surprise visit, Namor
issues a warning to Queen Ramonda and Princess Shuri that he will stop
at nothing to protect their countries' shared vibranium resource, now that
T'Challa has revealed its existence to the wider world.

Namor's forces abduct Shuri and engineering prodigy Riri Williams,
responsible for devising a vibranium detector used by the C.I.A. During
her time undersea, Shuri begins to understand Talokan culture and a
concept of what their shared protection of vibranium might look like.

Former Wakandan War Dog spy Nakia's rescue mission of Shuri and
Williams so enrages Namor that he declares war, and his Talokanil army
attacks Wakanda. Determined to recapture Williams, Namor floods the
throne room and Queen Ramonda dies saving Williams from drowning.
The royal palace—and its magnificent throne room—is just one of many
fine buildings laid waste by Namor's tidal wave of destruction.

17

Ceremonial Mask

Used by: M'Baku

Years in use: Unknown to the present day

This wooden mask is a relic of the Jabari Tribe from the Wakanda region of Africa. Its design is likely inspired by the primates native to the mountain highlands, the Jabari Tribe's traditional homeland.

After T'Chaka, King of Wakanda, is killed in a terrorist attack during the United Nations Sokovia Accords conference in Vienna in 2016, M'Baku, leader of the Jabari Tribe, wears this mask to challenge T'Chaka's son, T'Challa, for the vacant crown. While other Wakandan tribes are willing to accept T'Challa as the rightful heir to the throne, M'Baku calls for the invocation of ceremonial combat at Warrior Falls, a battle to the death to prove who is worthy to be king.

T'Challa wins the fight, but spares M'Baku and allows him to peacefully return to his mountain tribe. M'Baku later repays T'Challa's mercy and respect, saving T'Challa's life when he faces another challenge for the throne—this time from Erik Killmonger—which T'Challa fails. M'Baku allows T'Challa's family and loyalists to seek refuge in his village during Killmonger's brief, turbulent reign.

M'Baku proves his allegiance to T'Challa when he agrees to permit Jabari warriors to join the battles against Thanos that take place in 2018 and in the wake of 2023's Time Heist—the Avengers successful bid to bring back those who were lost to the Snap. M'Baku also stands with Wakanda after T'Challa's death, when the vibranium-rich country comes under attack from Namor's Talokanil forces. He supports T'Challa's sister Shuri in her role as the new Black Panther, but when Shuri chooses not to appear at the coronation ceremony at Warrior Falls he arrives in her place ready to challenge for the throne.

18

The Hulk's Skull Bed

Used by: Hulk

Years in use: 2015 to 2017

Following his wave of destruction during a battle with Iron Man in Johannesburg in 2015, the Hulk fled Earth in a flurry of guilt and landed on Sakaar. This planet had the dubious reputation of serving as the trash dump of the galaxy.

Captured by Sakaar's ruler, the Grandmaster, the Hulk became the star attraction in the autocrat's Contest of Champions. This gladiator-style arena competition provided entertainment for the mostly impoverished masses who lived in a polluted environment. Participants in the contest competed at the whim of the Grandmaster, who was wont to claim: "Any contender who defeats my champion, their freedom they shall win."

The Hulk soon proved himself an unbeatable champion, gaining considerable status in the Grandmaster's eyes. Between victories in the arena he reclined on an enormous bed fashioned from the skull of some massive creature. This impressive bed frame formed the centerpiece of his celebrity-level living quarters—which also included a hot tub, exercise equipment, and a not-so-mini minibar.

The skull bed provided the Hulk with a sinister-looking but comfortable space for the duration of his stay on Sakaar. This lasted until 2017, when his Avengers teammate Thor confronted the Hulk in the arena. After a bruising contest, Thor tried to enlist the Hulk and Valkyrie to defeat Hela, Goddess of Death, who had seized power on Asgard.

Eventually, Bruce Banner emerged from his two-year silence within the Hulk. Thor, Banner, and Valkyrie then embarked on a quest to defeat Hela and save Asgard's people.

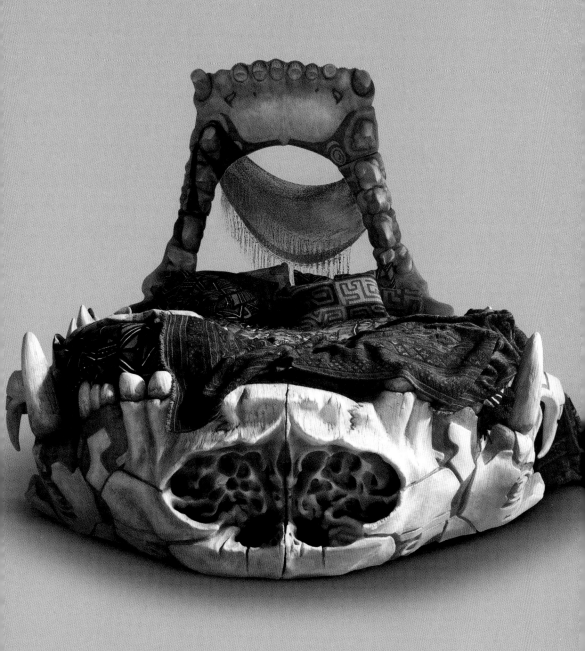

19

Scrapper Masks

Used by: Scavengers on Sakaar

Years in use: Unknown to the present day

These masks are representative of the diverse headgear worn by Scrappers, inhabitants of Sakaar, a planet that serves as the trash receptacle of the galaxy. Wormholes in space and time deposit all kinds of objects to this location, which becomes "the collection point for all lost and unloved things." Some of the living creatures deposited on Sakaar end up surviving as scavengers on the planet. Their garb reflects their varied cultural backgrounds, combined with materials that they have salvaged.

Only those residents of Sakaar that rise higher in service appear in more refined attire. They owe their privileges to the patronage of the autocratic, manipulative Grandmaster who rules the planet. Utterly selfish, the Grandmaster does not give his various servants names; instead he calls them by a number, such as Scrapper #142 (formerly known in Asgard as Valkyrie).

Scrappers' "recycle and reuse" method of clothing themselves adds to the striking diversity of their appearance. However, the most remarkable aspect of their ragged wardrobe is the wide variety of their masks, the purpose of which may be to protect themselves from the noxious atmosphere caused by the vast trash heaps littering Sakaar.

Scrappers also have some impressive weapons. A band of armed and masked Scrappers capture Thor in a high-tech net when he is dispatched to Sakaar by Hela's sorcery. To prevent the Scrappers using Thor—and her—for food, Scrapper #142 is forced to wipe out this marauding group.

Behind their masks, the mass of Scrappers eke out a miserable existence on the planet and are discontented with their lot. As soon as the Grandmaster's regime shows signs of weakness, they are ready to rise up. They seize their chance when Thor, Hulk, and Scrapper #142 break free of the Grandmaster's control and escape the planet that, up until now, no one has ever left.

The masks worn by Strappers give them sinister appearance.

20

3D Model of Ego's World

Used by: Ego
Years in use: Unknown to 2014

This large-scale diorama existed on the Celestial Ego's planet as a manifestation of the narration of his own history. It served as a visual representation of the story of his existence that Ego told his son Peter Quill (Star-Lord), Gamora, and Drax after he saved them from a mid-air ambush by their enemies, the Sovereign.

By means of this 3D model, Ego explained how the first thing he remembered was being adrift in the cosmos, utterly and entirely alone, and how over millions of years he learned to control the molecules around him, growing smarter and stronger. Ego described how he built everything around him, layer by layer, "including the very planet you walk on now" but how that was not enough to satisfy him. He only found meaning after he implanted thousands of extensions of himself on thousands of worlds. On Earth, he met and briefly fell in love with Peter's mother, Meredith.

Ego regaled Peter with how thrilled he was to find that his earthly son shared his immortal Celestial genes—his other offspring all failed in this respect and their bones formed a huge, gruesome pile. He dazzled Peter with the vision of how he could share in the legacy that would fulfill Ego's overarching dream: "To grow and spread, covering all that exists until everything is me!"

When Ego boasted that he was responsible for killing Peter's mother, however, Peter was enraged. Throwing off his father's hypnotic spell, he utterly rejected his seductive masterplan. Peter and his fellow Guardians of the Galaxy—including new addition Mantis—brought Ego's megalomaniac quest to an explosive end, obliterating both this Ego-centric model and the sentient planet on which Ego existed.

WESTVIEW

"Home: It's Where You Make It."

POPULATION

3,892

ELEVATION

203'

Information: AVAILABLE AT WESTVIEW PUBLIC LIBRARY

21

Westview Sign

Used by: Travelers in New Jersey

Years in use: Unknown to the present day

This roadside sign marks the point of entry to the small suburban town of Westview in the state of New Jersey. Home to a relatively small population (3,892 according to the sign), Westview literally falls off the Federal Bureau of Investigation's radar following Wanda Maximoff's "hexing" of the community in 2023.

Just weeks after Hulk's Snap returns Wanda and half of all life back into existence, Wanda drives into Westview without her beloved Vision in her newly restored life. Thanos' quest to claim the Mind Stone—a vital part of the synthezoid—has eliminated Vision from the planet.

Upon her arrival at the Westview property Vision purchased for himself and Wanda in their days of planning a bright future together, Wanda is so overtaken by heartache that she unleashes her Chaos Magic upon the entire community. Her mystical powers embrace all the residents of Westview against their will. In this way she creates a hidden-from-outsiders fantasy world, a new storyline for herself, in the form of the idyllic life that she and Vision planned to live out together. Her imaginary life—cast with live yet involuntarily compelled actors—plays out in ways that visually echo the happy days of her youth as nostalgically tied to rose-tinted memories of watching American TV sitcoms with her family in Sokovia.

Wanda's "WandaVision" episodes play out in stylistically retro scenes in which she and Vision are newlyweds and soon the parents of two boys. The series eventually flows into airwaves that the F.B.I. (outside of the Westview bubble) picks up and slowly infiltrates. Eventually, F.B.I. pressure and the strain of maintaining magical control over the town undermine Wanda's illusory world. The residents of Westview return to the unscripted reality of normal smalltown living, while Wanda's nosy neighbor, Agatha Harkness, thanks to her own witchy ways, tunes into Wanda's new role as The Scarlet Witch.

22

Deviant Turned to a Tree

Created by: Sersi

Date: 2021 to the present day

This tree is unlike any other tree grown on Earth. It was once a monstrous Deviant and took on its current form after it attacked Sersi and she transformed it during a battle in the Amazon jungle.

Sersi is one of the Eternals. These immortal heroes have been dispatched by the Celestials (the highest level of energy that forms a being in the galaxy) to protect humankind on Earth by eliminating the Deviants, a predatory species.

Sersi serves faithfully for 7,000 years of the planet's history, using her powers of transforming matter to help human beings—such as by turning dirt into water to help sustain farming efforts—and by battling Deviants. The Eternals work toward their intended task with full compliance on Earth until they realize that Celestials only seek to keep planets in balance so that they can eventually grow new Celestials. Upon the Emergence of a new Celestial, the host planet explodes. Arishem, the Prime Celestial, informs Sersi that an Emergence is about to begin on Earth. Sersi laments that everyone on Earth will die, but Arishem explains that if the process of creating new Celestials does not continue the entire universe will be plunged into darkness and all life in it will be destroyed. Arishem also says that it was he that created the Deviants, "the same way that I created you." The Prime Celestial then appoints Sersi the Eternals' new leader, responsible for bringing the Emergence to fruition. Having come to care deeply for all intelligent life on Earth, Sersi doubts her duty to end it —unlike her fellow Eternal and lover, Ikaris. Eventually she chooses to sacrifice a Celestial to save the people of Earth. Arishem whisks her away from the planet she loves and says that her memories will show whether Earth's people are worthy to live. He will return for judgment.

23

Doctor Strange Statue

Seen by: Citizens of New York-838, 616-Doctor Strange, America Chavez
Years in use: Unknown to the present day (Universe-838)

This statue proudly stands in front of the main entryway to the New York Sanctum in Universe-838. The plaque on it reads: "Dr. Stephen Strange gave his life defeating Thanos. We express eternal gratitude to Earth's Mightiest Hero." Thanks to America Chavez's instinctive, but uncontrolled, Multiversal powers, the Doctor Strange of Universe-616 encounters this memorial in Universe-838—much to his surprise.

Taken captive for being a potential incursion threat in this particular universe, 616-Doctor Strange is brought before the Illuminati, protectors of Universe-838. He learns that the memorial to Doctor Strange is merely a sop to the public. The Illuminati believe that the populace needed a hero to admire instead of the truth that their Doctor Strange's meddling had caused an appalling tragedy. 838-Doctor Strange had used the powers of the *Darkhold*, the Book of the Damned, and partaken in Dreamwalking—a *Darkhold* spell that enabled the spellcaster to inhabit other versions of themselves thoughout the Multiverse—in a failed attempt to defeat Thanos. In the process, 838-Doctor Strange had caused an incursion that had wiped out an entire universe resulting in the deaths of countless innocent beings. It was not until 838-Doctor Strange renounced the *Darkhold* and helped the Illuminati find the *Book of Vishanti* that Thanos was finally defeated. However, a final threat to Multiversal security remained: 838-Doctor Strange himself. Forced to face the consequences of his devastating actions, he agreed to his own execution.

The Illuminati soon discover, to their cost, a far greater threat to the Multiverse than 616-Doctor Strange is at large—The Scarlet Witch. Leader of the Illuminati Professor X decides to trust 616-Doctor Strange and let him seek the *Book of Vishanti* in order to counter The Scarlet Witch's Dreamwalking rampage through the Multiverse.

24

Monster Hunter Medallion

Used by: Elite monster hunters, including Jack Russell

Years in use: Unknown to the present day

This impressive medallion is a mark of honor for monster hunters who have earned a prestigious level of kills, enough to be contenders to carry on the work of Ulysses Bloodstone, a legend in the realm of such "death dealing," as they have been known to call their work. Being conspicuous, the medallion is usually not worn when the hunters are out on their stealthy missions, but it is worthy of display on special occasions, such as when they are invited to gather at Bloodstone Manor.

The deep red jewel that forms the eye of the monstrous head depicted on the medallion is reminiscent of the Bloodstone. Monster hunters covet this powerful gem and weapon because it grants strength, protection, and longevity to those who possess it—assuming they are not a monster themselves, as the Bloodstone has a negative effect upon such creatures. Neither the medallion nor the Bloodstone is automatically bequeathed to the heir of the Bloodstone family, as Elsa Bloodstone can attest. She has neither in her possession when she participates in a deadly contest at Bloodstone Manor to determine who is worthy of holding the Bloodstone following the death of her father.

On the night of the contest, Elsa and a group of elite monster hunters are tasked with killing a monster to which the Bloodstone has been attached. All of those possessing medals meet bloody ends, except for one—Jack Russell—who helps Elsa win the prize and her place as Ulysses' true successor. It appears that all of Ulysses' formidable hunting skills have been inherited by his daughter, although not practiced by her for decades.

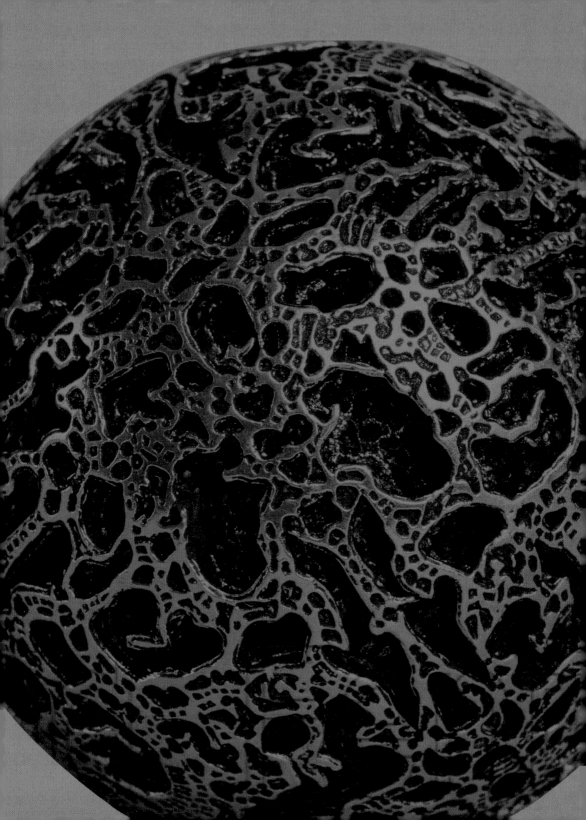

Mystical Might

These powerful relics almost defy understanding, exerting an influence and presence nearly unimaginable to the human mind—except that they have been imagined and exist within the Marvel Cinematic Universe. A sentient cape, a sword that controls passage between realms, and a gauntlet that can grant the wearer whatever they desire are just a few of the artifacts displayed in this section, fittingly titled "Mystical Might."

25

The Casket of Ancient Winters

Used by: Laufey, Loki

Years in use: The distant past to 2017

This relic was formerly owned by Laufey, King of the Frost Giants in the icy realm of Jotunheim. The Casket of Ancient Winters was an elegant container framed in silver-toned metal that emitted a blue glow through its ornate, crystal-like side panels. However, in the wrong hands, this artifact could create chilling havoc. It possessed the power to plunge a planet into an apocalyptic ice age.

When Laufey attempted to employ this weapon on Earth in 965 CE, the Asgardians led by Odin intervened. After defeating Laufey and his Frost Giant army in a battle at Tønsberg in Norway, Odin confiscated the casket. He also took pity on Laufey's abandoned baby son Loki, and brought the child back to his palace in Asgard to raise as his own son.

Upon its arrival in Asgard, the Casket of Ancient Winters was set upon a pedestal within Odin's vault, a hallowed place that housed a variety of treasures Odin had gained in various conquests.

Many years later, in 2010, the adult Loki crafted a vengeful plan to offer Laufey the return of the casket, only to trick and kill his birth father for abandoning him as a baby. With Odin slumbering in Odinsleep, Loki took control of Asgard and employed the Casket of Ancient Winters to freeze Heimdall and the Bifrost. He then dispatched the Destroyer automaton to kill Thor on Earth. Fortunately, this murderous scheme, like many of Loki's best-laid plans, ultimately failed.

The Casket of Ancient Winters was restored to its place in Odin's vault until its presumed demise in 2017 during Ragnarok—the massive destruction of Asgard wrought by the demonic Surtur.

26

The Eternal Flame Chalice

Used by: Odin, Hela, Surtur, Loki

Years in use: The distant past to 2017

The Eternal Flame is best known for its role in the prophecy of Ragnarok, the fated destruction of Asgard. The Eternal Flame's unquenchable, fiery essence flickered in a golden, chalice-like bowl set upon an ornate stand in a vault deep in Odin's palace. How Odin came to possess it, however, remains unknown.

The Eternal Flame continued to burn without incident until 2017, when the search for the Infinity Stones became an urgent race for Thor against Thanos and his minions. During that quest, Thor discovered that Surtur still desired to bring the Ragnarok prophecy to fruition. For this to occur, Surtur's crown had to be immersed in the Eternal Flame. Thor managed to frustrate Surtur's scheme by stealing his crown and concealing it in the same palace treasure room where the Eternal Flame was kept.

Meanwhile, Hela, Goddess of Death, imprisoned for years by Odin for her ruthless, power-hungry disposition, was at large and gathering power now that her father was no longer alive. Her aim was to conquer every one of the Nine Realms, starting with Asgard.

Following Odin's death, Hela seized Asgard and, using the Eternal Flame, raised an army of dead warriors and the monstrous Fenris Wolf. Only the destruction of her power source—Asgard itself—could prevent her bringing death to every realm. To achieve the nullification of Hela, Loki combined Surtur's crown with the Eternal Flame, immediately unleashing Ragnarok. Asgard was consumed—a tragic but necessary end that scotched Hela's horrific ambitions. The fate of the Eternal Flame post-Ragnarok is a mystery.

27

Mjolnir

Used by: Odin, Hela, Thor, Captain America, Vision, Jane Foster
Years in use: The distant past to the present day

Mjolnir is a war hammer hewn from metal mined from the core of a dying star by dwarves on Nidavellir, one of the Nine Realms that were once under the protection of the Asgardians. Mjolnir is most recognized as Thor's weapon of choice and is essentially a family heirloom.

The legendary hammer was originally forged for Thor's father Odin and was also briefly utilized by Hela, Thor's older sister. As Odin explains to his son, "Mjolnir's power has no equal as a weapon to destroy, or as a tool to build. It is a fit companion for a king."

Mjolnir has been enchanted so that its powers can only be accessed by those worthy of its service, seemingly determined by Mjolnir itself. Those deemed unworthy are unable to lift or even move it—as Loki discovers when Thor uses the hammer to pin him down. The judicious nature of Mjolnir's receptiveness is no secret. It is clearly inscribed on the shaft of the hammer to read:

"WHOSOEVER HOLDS THIS HAMMER, IF HE BE WORTHY, SHALL POSSESS THE POWER OF THOR."

This engraved honor literally reflects the tight bond that Mjolnir has with Thor, who can draw Mjolnir to his hand upon his simple command. He later regrets the break of this bond when the mighty hammer no longer deems him worthy to wield it. This occurs when, after disobeying Odin and attacking the Frost Giants in Jotunheim, Thor is banished to Earth. In part thanks to his budding relationship with scientist Jane Foster, the previously hotheaded Thor begins to appreciate the virtues of humility and self-sacrifice and becomes worthy to wield Mjolnir once more.

The mystical powers of Mjolnir extend to controlling the weather, particularly violent thunderstorms, and providing its wielder with the capability of flight. Gripping the hammer's leather thong, Thor whirls Mjolnir at incredible speed to create a tornado when battling the Destroyer automaton on Earth. He also employs Mjolnir to emit coruscating lightning

Intricate designs on the corner panels of Mjolnir
hark back to ancient runes of the Asgardian
culture, symbology which has also carried
through into earthly Celtic and Norse imagery.

strikes during pulverizing attacks on the Chitauri during the Battle of New
York (2012). Thor's other notable battles with Mjolnir include confronting
the Marauders in the War of the Nine Realms (2013) and clashing with the
Dark Elves in the Battle of Greenwich (2013).

Mjolnir also enhances Thor's natural ability to leap to great heights by
working in a propeller mode, creating enough force to travel great
distances, as shown in Thor's battle with Malekith or when he evades a
falling S.H.I.E.L.D. prison cell.

Beyond members of the Odin family line, Mjolnir has only been enabled
in the hands of Captain America, Vision, and Jane Foster as The Mighty
Thor. Mjolnir's connection to Foster is founded upon her close relationship
with Thor, which dates back to 2014. Thor specifically asks Mjolnir to
always protect Foster.

On a few occasions the power of Mjolnir has seemingly been matched—
such as when Thor attempts to disarm the Tesseract and during a
confrontation with Captain America's vibranium shield. The shockwave
created when hammer and shield clash levels hundreds of acres of
surrounding forest.

Mjolnir is eventually destroyed by Hela in 2017. Its shattered remnants
are displayed as a tourist attraction in New Asgard, and Thor reluctantly
moves on to a new signature weapon, the ax Stormbreaker.

Years later, however, Mjolnir mystically restores itself in order to support
Jane Foster in her role as The Mighty Thor. Sadly, being a human hero, not
a god like Thor, takes a heavy toll on her physical health, which is already
severely compromised by cancer.

Mjolnir also makes a special appearance while otherwise out of commission via time-travel. Thor traverses back in time to an alternate universe and then carries his beloved weapon forward into the Sacred Timeline so that Mjolnir can be utilized by Captain America against an alternate version of the Titan Thanos.

The hammer's mystical qualities are not confined to exhibitions of strength and power. Mjolnir has disguised itself as an umbrella in order to keep a low profile in the everyday world of Midgard. It has also delivered healing energy to Thor, such as after his brutal battle with the Destroyer.

After Jane Foster, The Mighty Thor, dies, Thor once again wields Mjolnir. His adopted daughter thinks it looks "boring" so she colorfully decorates one side of it.

The destroyed Mjolnir was on display as a relic exhibit in New Asgard for a short while, until it sensed a new calling and restored itself to support The Mighty Thor, Jane Foster.

28

Heimdall's Sword

Used by: Heimdall, Loki, Skurge
Years in use: The distant past to 2018

This magnificent blade was best known for supporting the watch and duty of Heimdall, the all-seeing and revered gatekeeper of Asgard's Bifrost. Its greatest power was its role as the key that opened the Bifrost, the principal gateway between the Nine Realms of Yggdrasil—and beyond.

Heimdall's mighty sword was also a formidable, weighty weapon with a two-handed grip. With slashing strokes, Heimdall used it to make short work of an invading band of Frost Giants attempting to kill Odin. He subsequently employed the weapon to destroy a Dark Elves' ship when Asgard came under attack.

Heimdall's sword was a vital tool in the spread of Asgardian influence across the cosmos, and it served the realms well when in Heimdall's possession. He used the blade to activate a defensive shield over Asgard

during the Dark Elf conflict, until Thor was able to end the attack by defeating the Dark Elves' leader Malekith during a battle in Greenwich, London in 2013.

At times during its existence, the sword unfortunately fell into the possession of unscrupulous figures. In 2010, Loki used the Casket of Ancient Winters to freeze Heimdall in a block of ice. He then employed the sword to access the Bifrost and send the Destroyer automaton to Earth in an attempt to eliminate Thor.

After Thor refused to accept the throne of Asgard, Loki impersonated Odin, took control of the realm, and banished Heimdall. The sword was placed in the hands of Skurge, an unprincipled warrior who briefly became the gatekeeper of the Bifrost.

Skurge utilized the sword in support of interplanetary theft in 2017, stealing mementos from Midgard such as a Vespa motor scooter, a Shake Weight dumbbell, and two M16A1 assault rifles that he named "Des" and "Troy." Heimdall's sword was presumed destroyed when Thanos and the Children of Thanos attacked the spaceship *Statesman* during the Titan's quest to gather the six Infinity Stones and wipe out half of the universe's life-forms.

29

Loki's Scepter

Used by: Loki, Hydra, Tony Stark, Bruce Banner
Years in use: 2012 to 2015

Gifted to Loki by the Titan Thanos, the scepter is made from unknown metals. It comprises a long, extendable handle and double blades that surround a glowing blue orb enclosed in a black case. Loki carried the scepter during his 2012 invasion of Earth when he entered via a portal in the Project Pegasus laboratory within the NASA/S.H.I.E.L.D. joint Dark Mission Facility.

The scepter wields force in multiple ways. As a simple weapon, Loki uses its sharp blades to stab or impale victims—as the brave S.H.I.E.L.D. Agent Phil Coulson tragically discovers. He also uses it to bludgeon opponents. More significantly, the mystical energy contained within its glowing gem can be directed and fired, with devastating effect.

The scepter also channels its energy to create a force field as a barrier from projectiles such as bullets. Most intriguingly, the scepter can subtly convey its energy into a living being, achieving a mind-controlling effect— as proven by the uncharacteristic behavior of Dr. Erik Selvig, Agent Clint Barton, and others selected by Loki. The scepter's mind-controlling capabilities do not necessarily require direct contact with a victim; they also appear to work when the artifact is in close proximity, as shown when its presence creates tension between Steve Rogers and Tony Stark, and agitation in Bruce Banner. Additionally, the scepter serves as a mental conduit between Loki and the Other, Thanos' loyal servant, even when there is considerable physical distance between them.

With this scepter in hand, Loki leads Thanos' invasion force of Chitauri to Earth. This incident results in the formation of the Avengers to defend the planet and exposes the general public on Earth to life beyond their planet on a large scale for the first time. In the wake of this failed invasion, Loki's scepter is confiscated by S.H.I.E.L.D. for study.

The artifact is later appropriated by Hydra during its infiltration of S.H.I.E.L.D.'s elite S.T.R.I.K.E. unit and brought to its research base in Sokovia. A series of harmful experiments results, involving human specimens such as Wanda and Pietro Maximoff and weapons technology,

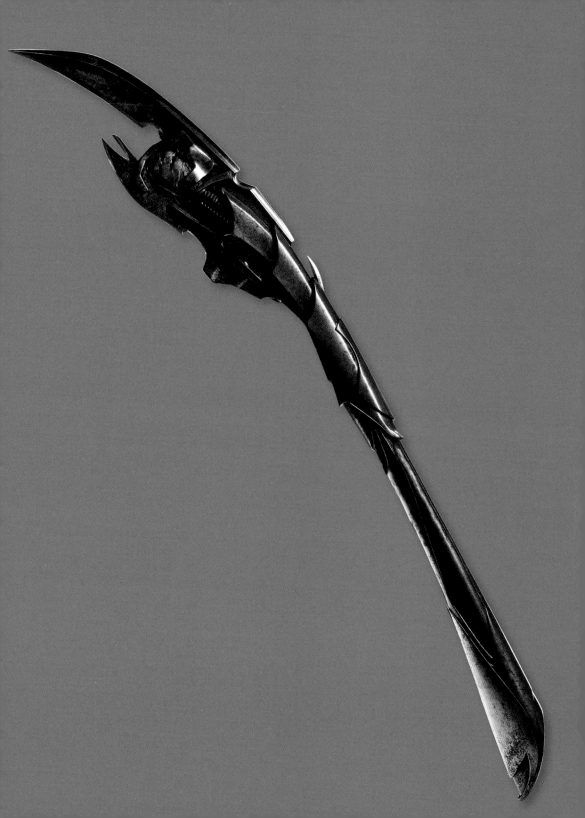

under the orders of Baron Wolfgang von Strucker.

The Avengers later reclaim the scepter from Hydra for scientist Bruce Banner and inventor Tony Stark's study. Stark's A.I. assistant JARVIS identifies that the scepter is of alien origin and that its blue orb is the protective housing for "something inside." Furthermore, Banner and Stark detect the presence of neurons, as if the object was thinking. The two scientists decide to tap into the scepter's power for Stark's Ultron Program, hitherto little more than a fantasy. By harnessing the power inherent in the

scepter with his robotics knowledge, Stark hopes to create an Iron Legion of robots to bring "peace in our time," easing the pressure on the Avengers. Stark's and Banner's efforts are hijacked by Ultron's artificial intelligence. Ultron views the Avengers—and humanity in general—as the supreme threat to Earth's continued survival and resolves to annihilate both of them.

The Ultron line of experimentation leads to the discovery of the core of the scepter being the Mind Stone, one of the six Infinity Stones that predate the universe. Ultron uses the Mind Stone from the scepter to power up a synthezoid body for himself.

The fate of the scepter from that point on has not been recorded.

The scepter's Mind Stone glows with ominous power in Stark's lab.

Tony Stark and Bruce Banner
seek to understand the mysteries
contained in Loki's scepter.

For a short while, the Mind Stone serves as the power source for a
synthezoid being of artificial intelligence known as Vision, until Thanos
once again seeks possession of it as part of his goal to reunite the Infinity
Stones. He finally achieves this goal following the battle in Wakanda in
2018, leading to a detrimental effect far greater than any damage the
original scepter had caused: the onset of the Snap and the elimination
of half of all the life in the universe.

30

Surtur's Crown

Used by: Surtur, Loki
Years in use: The distant past to 2017

This crown is the possession of the fire demon Surtur. The metal-hewn half-skull artifact is adorned with antlers that echo the adornments worn by other powerful royal beings in the Nine Realms such as Loki and Hela. Its origin can be traced back to the fiery realm of Muspelheim, and its final appearance is on Asgard, at the onset of Ragnarok.

Surtur desired vengeance against Odin for centuries after he was conquered by the dynamically destructive pairing of Odin and his daughter Hela, Goddess of Death, during their early quest to bring all Nine Realms under Asgard's rule.

In 2017, Surtur is made aware of Thor Odinson's search for the Infinity Stones, and stalls that effort by imprisoning Thor. During his incarceration, Thor comes to understand that Surtur's hatred for Asgard still smolders. Surtur longs to fulfill his destiny and bring about Ragnarok, the destruction of Asgard, by uniting his crown with the Eternal Flame, which Odin keeps in his palace vault.

With the help of his trusty hammer Mjolnir, Thor knocks the crown from Surtur's head and escapes Muspelheim with it. He later adds the crown to the collection of mystical artifacts in Odin's palace.

Following Odin's death, Hela takes control of Asgard and, using the Eternal Flame, raises an army of dead warriors to support her latest bid for control of the Nine Realms. Thor realizes that only the complete revival of the fire demon and the onset of Ragnarok can block Hela's efforts. After coming to this grim but inevitable conclusion, Loki and Thor combine forces against their power-hungry sister. Thor sends Loki to reunite Surtur's crown with the Eternal Flame, releasing the awesome power of Surtur, who unleashes Ragnarok, turning Asgard into a blazing wasteland.

31

The Cloak of Levitation

Used by: Doctor Strange
Years in recent use: 2016 to the present day

The Cloak of Levitation is a magical relic housed in the New York Sanctum collection of the Masters of the Mystic Arts. Finished with embroidered edges and lined with a checkered print, the cloak is resplendent with decorative gold clasps with ruby inlay.

At first sight, the cloak appears a soft, fancy, even delicate fashion accessory. However, this charismatic item of clothing is far more robust than might be expected and its powers are impressive. The cloak has the ability to fly and to hover, protecting its wearer while it bears him aloft, sometimes at great speed, and to considerable heights.

The cloak's human bearer is the formerly renowned neurosurgeon Dr. Stephen Strange. After a car accident cripples his hands, Dr. Strange makes his way to Kamar-Taj in Kathmandu, Nepal, to heal himself.

There, under the tutelage of Sorceror Supreme the Ancient One, he becomes Doctor Strange, a Master of the Mystic Arts and the protector of the New York Sanctum. When he enters the sanctum, the cloak jumps into action to enclose its chosen partner and help him defend himself against an attack by villainous sorcerer Kaecilius and his Zealots. This is just the first of many instances in which Doctor Strange and the Cloak of Levitation counter otherworldly threats in Multiversal space with a combination of magical charms and combat skills.

Time and again, the cloak has affirmed its loyalty to Doctor Strange. Even when it changes color and size in alternate realities, the cloak's allegiance has remained constant, most notably when it chooses to perish over and over with Strange while battling Dormammu, demonic ruler of the Dark Dimension. At times, the Cloak of Levitation almost seems to act like Doctor Strange's conscience—as exemplified by its high standards of behavior and decision-making when Doctor Strange falls under the influence of the malign book of spells called the *Darkhold*.

32

The Book of Cagliostro

Used by: The Ancient One, Doctor Strange, Kaecilius
Years in use: Unknown to the present day

This ancient tome contains some of the most powerful spells collected in the library of the Masters of the Mystic Arts. *The Book of Cagliostro*, so named for the entity that originally gathered and transcribed spells into his own library and books, is held in a restricted access collection within the Kamar-Taj, the temple-like central location and training ground of those welcomed to practice the Mystic Arts. This particular book is only accessible to more practiced Masters such as the Ancient One because improper use of its rituals, especially those that connect to the Dark Dimension, may lead to devastating consequences. For example, in 2016, Master Kaecilius and his Zealots bring about dire complications during their unsanctioned efforts to use *The Book of Cagliostro* to summon the power of the Dark Dimension and its power-hungry ruler Dormammu, who desires to rule all the dominions in the Multiverse, including Earth.

Kaecilius excels as a student at Kamar-Taj but, proud and headstrong, is unsatisfied with the level of teaching, claiming that the Ancient One only gives students "parlor tricks" and keeps the real magic for herself. He wants to gain more mystical power and to gain it faster. He particularly yearns to acquire immortality by accessing the Dark Dimension, a place beyond time. He tells Doctor Strange, "Time is the true enemy of us all. Time kills everything."

The Ancient One refuses to permit other students access to other dimensions, but Kaecilius discovers that the Ancient One has secretly accessed the Dark Dimension in order to gain immortality. In company with a group of like-minded students, who become known as his Zealots, Kaecilius takes drastic action.

Convinced that communicating with the realm of Dormammu, demon ruler of the Dark Dimension, is the path to gaining immortality and

Pages of *The Book of Cagliostro,* featuring an illustration of the Eye of Agamotto.

defeating the "slavery" of time, and thus death itself, they overpower and behead the Kamar-Taj's head librarian in order to steal the pages of *The Book of Cagliostro* that will grant them access to the Dark Dimension.

In their haste to summon Dormammu, however, Kaecilius and his Zealots do not obtain the pages of *The Book of Cagliostro* that explain the ramifications of casting spells to open the Dark Dimension. The effect is to cause ripples in the Mirror Dimension. In that dimension, Kaecilius discovers that the laws of gravity, physics, and matter are all pliable. His learned ability to manipulate matter outside of the Mirror Dimension further demonstrates the dangers of dabbling in the arcane mysteries of *The Book of Cagliostro.*

Kaecilius and his Zealots destroy the London Sanctum of the Masters of the Mystic Arts and, later, the Hong Kong Sanctum. By these actions, Kaecilius breaks mystically powered barriers and helps pave the way for Dormammu to enter the earthly dimension and channel power into Kaecilius' efforts to gain immortality. Such ramifications are somewhat understood in advance by Doctor Strange as he seeks to offset the damage caused by Kaecilius' mystical meddling.

Strange has already gained knowledge of how to utilize the Eye of Agamotto to manipulate time, so he is able to travel back and discover what Kaecilius has done by reading the stolen pages of *The Book of Cagliostro* himself before Kaecilius removed them. Strange undertakes this task knowing that the implementation of such time travel spells can trigger time loops, dimensional portals, and spatial paradoxes—all of which he must traverse in order to counteract Kaecilius' plans.

Fortunately Strange's innate—but previously untested—talents for practicing the mystic arts allow him to quickly adapt to the new challenges that he encounters in space and time, including vanquishing one of Kaecilius' Zealots on the Astral Plane. He also battles Kaecilius and his Zealots in a Mirror Dimensional New York City.

Finally, by using spells in the missing pages of *The Book of Cagliostro*, Strange enters the hitherto timeless Dark Dimension and uses the Eye of Agamotto to trap Dormammu in a time loop. Dormammu agrees to leave Earth in peace to escape the time loop and preserve his Dark Dimension.

The all-important
missing pages.

33

The Orb

Used by: The Guardians of the Galaxy, Ronan the Accuser, Thanos
Years in use: The distant past to 2018

The Orb is an intricately wrought, metal-like, spherical structure in which the Power Stone, one of the six Infinity Stones, was contained for many years, mainly within a temple on the planet Morag. The device was seemingly crafted to keep the Power Stone from coming into direct contact with any life-forms. Tides on Morag kept the Orb hidden for added protection against misuse of the Power Stone.

The Titan Thanos instructs Kree warlord Ronan the Accuser to find the Orb. However, Star-Lord Peter Quill steals the artifact, in the process double-crossing the Ravagers crime syndicate led by Yondu. These brigands have been tasked by the Broker to obtain the Orb for Taneleer Tivan, whose hoard of relics has earned him the soubriquet the Collector.

Ronan dispatches the assassin Gamora to obtain the Orb, and she and Quill clash on the planet Xandar, a confrontation also involving bounty hunters Rocket and Groot. The Orb is confiscated by Xandar's Nova Corps, but Quill, Gamora, Rocket, and Groot, joined by Drax the Destroyer, reclaim it and decide to sell the Orb to the Collector themselves.

An accidental triggering of the Power Stone destroys much of the Collector's collection. Realizing the stone's power, Quill and his crew depart Xandar with the Orb, only to be overtaken by Ronan, who wants the Power Stone to destroy the Xandarians, long-time enemies of the Kree. His possession of the stone leads to massive destruction on Xandar before Quill's crew, calling themselves the Guardians of the Galaxy, recover the Orb and use the Power Stone to kill Ronan. They then return the Orb to the Nova Corps for safekeeping.

The Orb is later seized by Thanos, who combines the Power Stone with the other Infinity Stones in the Infinity Gauntlet. With a click of his fingers, he initiates the Snap, fulfilling his goal of eliminating half of all life-forms in the universe. Following this incident, the Orb's whereabouts are unknown, despite a time-traveling expedition into the past undertaken by the Avengers to reverse the Snap.

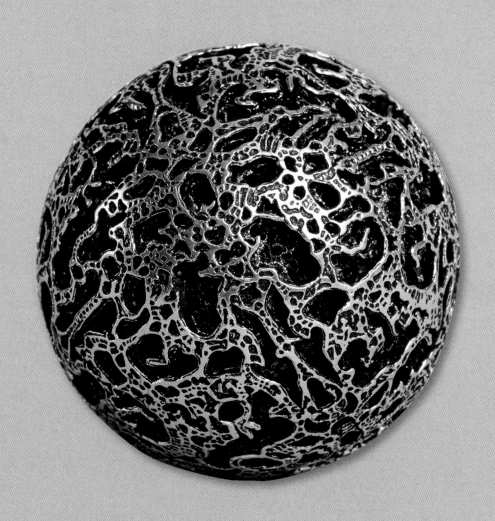

34

Sling Ring

Used by: Doctor Strange, Ned Leeds, Spider-Man
Years in recent use: 2017 to the present day

The sling ring is a powerful accessory worn by Masters of the Mystic Arts to open circular portals into other locations or dimensions. The dual-digit ring is worn on the left hand, upon the second and third fingers. When that hand is elevated and the right hand makes a counterclockwise motion, the sorcerer is able to open a gateway as visualized. Each sling ring is unique. The golden device featured here belongs to Doctor Strange, and has been used time and again for travel through the Multiverse.

Doctor Strange learns to master his sling ring after a tough yet effective lesson by the Ancient One—she teleports the novitiate Doctor Strange to the freezing summit of Mount Everest and leaves him there with just a sling ring to make his way back to the warmth and safety of the Kamar-Taj training facility. His mastery of the sling ring subsequently proves vital to thwarting Loki's efforts to cause mayhem in the New York Sanctum in 2017, quickly transporting Loki off the New York streets and later to Norway.

In 2018, Doctor Strange employs his sling ring multiple times in a battle in lower Manhattan, facing Children of Thanos Ebony Maw and Cull Obsidian who are seeking the Time Stone, protected by the Masters of the Mystic Arts. The sling ring aids victory by transporting Iron Man into the battle and the enraged Hulk out of it.

Later that year, in a battle on Titan, Doctor Strange uses his sling ring to facilitate Mantis' attempt to hypnotize Thanos and prevent him adding the final Infinity Stone—the Mind Stone—to the Infinity Gauntlet. This effort ultimately fails; Thanos snaps his fingers and causes half of all life in the universe—including Doctor Strange himself—to disappear from existence.

Doctor Strange's sling ring was briefly utilized by Ned Leeds, who accidentally summoned multiple Spider-Men from the Multiverse; it was also possessed by Spider-Man for a short while after interaction in the Multiverse, specifically within the Mirror Dimension in 2024, but later recovered by Doctor Strange.

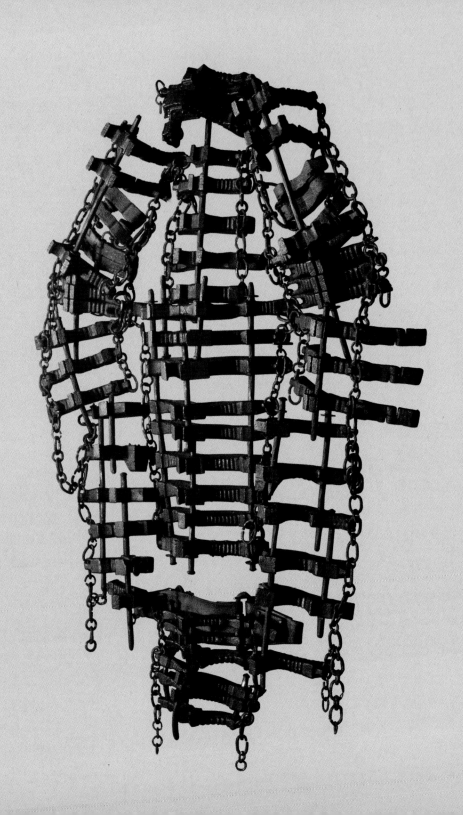

35

The Crimson Bands of Cyttorak

Used by: Masters of the Mystic Arts, Doctor Strange
Years in use: The distant past to the present day

The Crimson Bands of Cyttorak were a multi-part artifact constructed from an unknown metal. This ancient restraining device was housed in the New York Sanctum under the curatorship of the Masters of the Mystic Arts.

The Crimson Bands' presence in that location was fortunate. In 2017, the Sanctum came under attack by the traitorous Master Kaecilius and his band of Zealots, acting as servants of Dormammu, the ruler of the Dark Dimension. A new student of the Mystic Arts, Doctor Strange found himself forced to battle this more experienced Master. However, with the guidance of another Sanctum artifact, the Cloak of Levitation, Doctor Strange was able to utilize the Crimson Bands of Cyttorak to entrap Kaecilius and pause his path of destruction. While Kaecilius was trapped by the device, he informed Doctor Strange of his plans to hand the world to Dormammu, ruler of the Dark Dimension, a place beyond time. "We can all live forever," he declared. "Humanity longs for the eternal."

The combined forces of Kaecilius' Zealots broke the the Crimson Bands' mystical grip, freeing Kaecilius and allowing him to pursue his goal of empowering Dormammu. Doctor Strange returned to the Sanctum to find the Crimson Bands smashed to pieces.

Doctor Strange's use of the original Crimson Bands to confine an enemy may have inspired him—now far more practiced in the Mystic Arts—during the Avengers' struggle against Thanos for possession of the Infinity Stones. In the course of that epic battle, Doctor Strange conjured a magical force that restrained Thanos' left arm bearing the Infinity Gauntlet with bands of crimson energy—for a short while, at least.

36

The Infinity Gauntlet

Used by: Thanos
Year in use: 2018

The Infinity Gauntlet is a powerful artifact specifically designed to house and harness the energies of the six Infinity Stones that were created during the Big Bang. These stones are individually known as the Space, Reality, Power, Mind, Soul, and Time Stones. In its physical form, the Infinity Gauntlet is a golden glove worn on the left hand, adorned with intricate detailing, with individual compartments hewn to hold one each of the Infinity Stones. The gauntlet seems to possess a magnetic quality, as the stones do not require to be placed in their intended nooks but rather float and fuse into place when in close proximity to the gauntlet. The order of stone placement on the back of the gauntlet is Soul-Reality-Space-Power from left to right just below the fingers; the Time Stone is housed below the thumb; and the Mind Stone sits in the center of the back of the gauntlet. When all six stones are set in their compartments, the Infinity Gauntlet becomes a weapon of unparalleled power, able to dramatically alter reality itself following a moment of meditation and a snap of the fingers from the mighty being capable of wielding the artifact.

The creation of the Infinity Gauntlet is traceable back to Thanos, who forces Eitri of Nidavellir to craft the unique object from the same forge that fired other great weapons, such as Mjolnir for Thor. In an effort to protect that power, Thanos proceeds to eliminate all of the Dwarves on Nidavellir except Eitri, and extinguish their forge after he obtains the precious gauntlet so that another comparable weapon cannot be made with the Dwarves' well-proven metal-working skills. In that lethal sweep of Nidavellirian life, Thanos spares Eitri so that he may testify to the terrible power of Thanos. Eitri's remaining solitary life is to be lived with hands damaged by Thanos to prevent him crafting future weapons.

Thanos portrays his ambition to possess the Infinity Gauntlet and all its stones as a method—albeit a drastic one—of establishing balance and order in the universe; however, this involves removing half of all life from

existence. The Avengers and their allies are desperate to prevent Thanos obtaining all the Infinity Stones and harnessing such extreme cosmic power. The heroes travel to Wakanda in a last desperate attempt to prevent Thanos from gaining the final stone—the Mind Stone. They are joined by the Wakandan army and battle Thanos' mighty forces, which include the Children of Thanos. The appearance of Thanos himself proves too much for the combined might of the Avengers. The Scarlet Witch attempts to destroy the Mind Stone, but Thanos simply uses the Time Stone to nullify her efforts.

With the acquisition of the Mind Stone—and the resultant death of Vision—Thanos' mission is almost complete. In a last desperate bid to stop the Titan, Thor hurls Stormbreaker at him. It strikes Thanos in the chest and not the head, and Thanos shrugs off the injury thanks to the power of the Infinity Gauntlet.

Thanos experiences a massive surge of energy as he prepares to fulfill his dream. He then simply snaps his fingers while envisioning his ideal universe. Numerous heroes are immediately removed from existence, including Black Panther, Falcon, The Scarlet Witch, Doctor Strange, Spider-Man, all the Guardians of the Galaxy except for Rocket, Nick Fury, Maria Hill, Hope Pym, Hank Pym, and Janet Van Dyne. For those who survive, this shattering cosmic event is written into history in 2018 as the Snap. Thanos then vanishes through a portal created for him by the Space Stone.

The Infinity Gauntlet suffers damage during the Snap owing to the immense flow of power it emits, but it is still functional enough for Thanos to use it to heal injuries he received fighting the Avengers and, more impactfully, to then destroy the stones themselves to prevent future drastic cosmic events. After this tremendous task, the Infinity Gauntlet is permanently fused to Thanos' left hand. The Avengers subsequently track Thanos down on another world, where he is living the peaceful life of a farmer. The formerly unstoppable Titan offers no resistance. Thor decapitates him with Stormbreaker, but the effects of the Snap remain.

Determined to somehow reverse the Snap, the remaining Avengers embark on a time-traveling mission via a Quantum Tunnel to retrieve the Infinity Stones from different points in history and alter Thanos' future actions. For this quest, Tony Stark, Bruce Banner, and Rocket construct the Nano Gauntlet, a new version of the Infinity Gauntlet. The Hulk, owing to his tolerance for gamma radiation, bravely agrees to wear it, well aware that its power could kill him. Fortunately, Hulk's version of the Snap proves successful in restoring the many lives lost in Thanos' Snap.

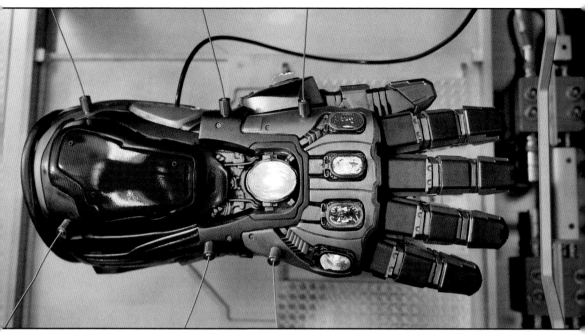

The new version of the Infinity Gauntlet created by the Avengers in hopes of reversing the Snap.

The stones throb with enormous power in the Avengers' Nano Gauntlet, which Hulk wears on his right hand.

37

The Necrosword

Used by: Gorr

Years in use: The distant past to 2025

This Necrosword was believed to be as old as the universe itself. The legendary weapon had proven powerful enough to slay gods, but was as devastating to those who possessed it as to those who fell beneath its blade. The Necrosword had an established pattern of utterly corrupting and destroying those who wielded it. It then fell into the hands of another individual who deemed themself capable of using it—an ambitious and ultimately fatal decision.

The Necrosword was last possessed by Gorr, who soon earned the soubriquet the God Butcher. Alone with his daughter on his devastated world, he prayed in vain to the god Rapu for help. After his daughter died, he came upon Rapu, who was celebrating killing the previous owner of the Necrosword. Mocked by Rapu and his supernatural friends, Gorr murdered Rapu with the Necrosword and embarked on a vendetta against all gods—a mission now empowered by having the Necrosword at his disposal.

With an army of shadow monsters, Gorr took the Necrosword on a rampage of god-killing until he aspired to conquer those affiliated with Asgard. To attract Thor's attention, he kidnapped the children of New Asgard—part of his plan to gain possession of Thor's mystical ax Stormbreaker, and open the Gates of Eternity. This would grant him access to the being Eternity who would grant his sole wish: the end of deities. Gorr was initially successful, defeating Thor with his forces, gaining possession of Stormbreaker and opening the Gates of Eternity. However the combined blows of Jane Foster—The Mighty Thor—and Thor himself destroyed the Necrosword and brought Gorr close to death.

Nevertheless, Gorr was about to make his final, god-destroying wish, when Thor begged him to reconsider and reflect on what he truly desired. As he died, Gorr finally rejected thoughts of mindless revenge and used his one wish to "seek love" by bringing his young daughter back to life. He then asked Thor to take care of her.

The end of the trail of darkness and destruction caused by Gorr and the Necrosword leads to a new path of light in the universe as navigated by the heroic team of Thor and his adopted daughter, who come to be known as Love and Thunder.

38

The Eye of Agamotto

Used by: Masters of the Mystic Arts, the Ancient One, Doctor Strange
Years in use: The ancient past to the present day

This powerful artifact has been handed down through generations of Masters of the Mystic Arts since the first Sorcerer Supreme, Agamotto, created and utilized it thousands of years ago. The main structure of the piece is a human-eye-shaped metallic cage hewn with a mix of golden and silver hues, embellished with carved designs that appear to be symbols from an ancient written language. The cage is worn as an amulet, to be hung around the wielder's neck on a strap made up of woven multicolored strands. The main chamber of the cage is designed to hold the Time Stone, one of the six Infinity Stones. This stone emits a green glow when activated.

Use of the Eye of Agamotto has been limited to advanced Masters, owing to the immense time-controlling powers that the Time Stone possesses. Written instructions for use of the Eye can be found within the pages of *The Book of Cagliostro*, an ancient collection of spells and other magical knowledge housed in a private collection within the library of Kamar-Taj, the training and learning grounds of the Masters, hidden away in Nepal. These instructions include the proper hand gestures that enable the wielder of this object to "open" the Eye, tap into the power of the Time Stone, and thus manipulate time itself.

The most recent sorcerer deemed worthy to utilize the powers of the Eye of Agamotto is Doctor Strange, whose skills are honed under the mentorship of the Sorcerer Supreme known as the Ancient One. Strange learns about the Eye when studying *The Book of Cagliostro* unattended one evening, practicing its power on an apple he is eating at the time. His meddling with the Eye's power leads to a further lesson from Masters Wong and Mordo about the dangers of time manipulation leading to branches in time, unstable dimensional openings, spatial paradoxes, and time loops.

After his mentor, the Ancient One, is defeated by a malign former student, Kaecilius, Doctor Strange is forced to put his learnings about the

Eye into play, employing a mix of Eye-empowered, spell-casting skills in his battles against Kaecilius and his Zealot followers in multiple dimensions. Strange uses the Eye of Agamotto to reverse time and counteract the destruction of the Hong Kong Sanctum, previously destroyed by Kaecilius.

Doctor Strange is eventually successful in defeating both Kaecilius and the greater threat that Kaecilius has unleashed, the so-called cosmic conqueror and destroyer of worlds, Dormammu. Doctor Strange uses the Eye to catch Dormammu in a time loop in the Dark Dimension, where time is not supposed to exist. Dormammu thus has no defense against Doctor Strange's ploy within his native realm, despite killing Doctor Strange over and over again.

In 2018, Strange's control of the Eye of Agamotto is put to the test when the Titan warlord Thanos seeks to eliminate half the living beings in the universe in order to create a more balanced existence, from his perspective. To do so, Thanos aims to control the Time Stone among the other Infinity Stones vital to achieving his devastating goal.

The Eye of Agamotto, housed on display in Kamar-Taj.

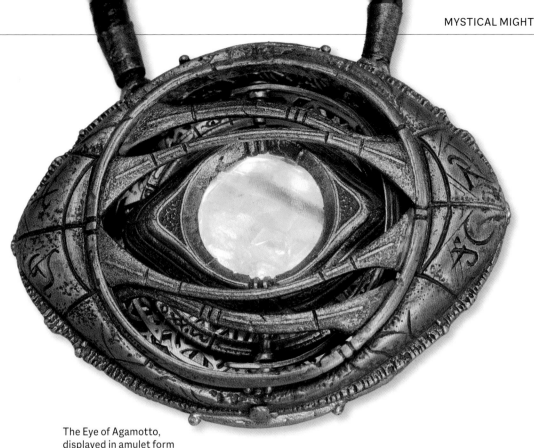

The Eye of Agamotto, displayed in amulet form and featuring the glowing Time Stone at its center.

Faced with this challenge, Strange uses the future-seeing powers of the Eye's central core to view more than 14 million possible outcomes during the ferocious battle to keep the Time Stone and the other Infinity Stones out of Thanos' hands. In alignment with the horrifying odds—14 million to one—that Doctor Strange witnesses in that future viewing effort, and after valiant battle alongside the Avengers, Strange loses the Time Stone to Thanos and seemingly the Eye as well.

39

The *Darkhold*

Used by: Magic wielders, The Scarlet Witch, Doctor Strange, Agatha Harkness
Years in use: The distant past to 2022

The *Darkhold* was also known as the Book of the Damned. It was a transcription of the dark magic spells Chthon, the first demon, engraved on the walls surrounding a throne he built atop Mount Wundagore as a place of power for The Scarlet Witch. Over the course of its long existence, the *Darkhold* was coveted by power-seeking individuals. The book changed hands often, corrupted those who used it, and created turmoil and destruction.

The *Darkhold* was constructed of archaic, paper-like pages, covered in a wrap decorated with stonework and metal. The book was a repository of Chaos Magic: its spells enabled practitioners to access energy from other dimensions and to Dreamwalk within the Multiverse by possessing their alternate selves in such spaces. However, these abilities came at a great cost.

This cost was unknown to the volume's possessor before a spell was wrought and varied according to the user. For example, when the Doctor Strange of another universe invoked *Darkhold* spells to rewind his history with former fiancée Christine Palmer, he turned sinister, his fingers turned black from touching the book, he caused an incursion in another dimension, and painfully grew a third eye.

When Wanda Maximoff sought the truth behind the *Darkhold*'s prophesy of her embodiment as The Scarlet Witch, it turned her fingers black and she developed an obsession with seeing and caring for her two children, Billy and Tommy, throughout the Multiverse.

Wanda eventually experienced qualms of conscience when she realized that in one universe her own children were afraid of her after she tried to replace the true version of their mother. She broke free from the *Darkhold*'s influence and turned the dark magic upon itself, seemingly destroying the *Darkhold* throughout the Multiverse so that others would be spared disaster.

40

The *Book of Vishanti*

Used by: Doctor Strange
Years in use: The distant past to 2024

While there are many spellbooks in the library of the Masters of the Mystic Arts in Kamar-Taj, Nepal, one very important tome remains elusive from even the highest level of sorcerer for a great period of history: the *Book of Vishanti*. This collection of wisdom grants great defensive powers to a sorcerer, in whatever manner they need to defeat an enemy. Doctor Strange first glimpses the *Book of Vishanti* in a dream that turns out to be prophetic: Dreamwalking in the Multiverse with a girl he will come to know as America Chavez, they are viciously attacked by a monster.

The book's true whereabouts remain a mystery until Doctor Strange and America Chavez come upon it in Universe-838 when seeking to defeat the plans of The Scarlet Witch. With the help of Strange's longtime colleague and companion Dr. Christine Palmer and the watch that she once gave him in the 838 timeline, the three are able to access the Gap Junction, a dreamlike realm in between worlds where the *Book of Vishanti* has resided for eons without disturbance. The book is an impressive sight, glowing with mystical energy and mounted upon a tall, ornate stand. They hope the mystical volume will help them counter the power of the *Darkhold* under which The Scarlet Witch operates.

Just after Doctor Strange removes the book from its holder, the Dreamwalking Scarlet Witch finds her way into the Gap Junction and unleashes a monstrous creature to destroy the *Book of Vishanti*. She then forces Chavez to open a portal back to her Wundagore mountain base, to extract Chavez's Multiversal powers for her own gain.

Luckily, the quick glance that Doctor Strange has at the book before it is reduced to ashes tells him that Chavez already possesses all the power she needs to defeat The Scarlet Witch. Doctor Strange follows their trail to Wundagore and inspires Chavez to do just that. Chavez manages to bring The Scarlet Witch back in touch with her Wanda-based humanity by showing her what a monster she has become through the eyes of her beloved sons. The power of the *Darkhold* is overcome, albeit at the cost of the precious *Book of Vishanti*.

41

The Scarab of Ammit

Used by: Ammit, Marc Spector, Steven Grant, Arthur Harrow, Layla El-Faouly
Years in use: The ancient past to the present day

The Scarab of Ammit is a powerful and beautiful relic that also serves as a compass. In the realm of Egyptian history and culture, the scarab is far more than just a dung beetle—it is a symbol of rebirth, renewal, resurrection, and protection in the afterlife. Its symbology has adorned jewelry, art, and funereal accessories for centuries.

The Scarab of Ammit is golden in color, made of an unknown metal, and inscribed with hieroglyphs. Its retractable wings are not used for flight—they protrude when the scarab activates as a compass. The artifact guides followers to the location of Ammit's spirit—revealed to be a ushabti figurine buried in the long-hidden tomb of Alexander the Great.

Alexander served as an avatar for the deity Ammit, championing her objective to eliminate potentially evil humans from the world, even before they committed any crime. Rival deities trapped Ammit following Alexander's death and buried her so that her efforts would cease. However, a modern disciple of Ammit, Arthur Harrow, seeks to use the scarab to locate and resurrect her. Relic hunter Marc Spector and museum worker Steven Grant—who inhabit the same human body via a dissociative personality disorder—aim to block Harrow's mission, for they are avatars of Khonshu, the Egyptian moon god who casts his wrath only upon those who actually harm the innocent.

An international chase leads to the scarab changing hands a number of times, leading Harrow, Spector/Grant and Spector's wife Layla El-Faouly to the tomb of Alexander the Great and causing Ammit's release from the figurine. A great battle among spirits and avatars follows that reveals Spector as Moon Knight, Grant as Mr. Knight, and El-Faouly as the Scarlet Scarab. Together they contain Ammit once again.

42

The Scales of Justice

Used by: Taweret

Years in use: The ancient past to the present day

The Scales of Justice are utilized by the ancient Egyptian goddess Taweret in her realm of the afterlife. The alters of fearless relic-hunter Marc Spector and fearful museum gift-shop worker Steven Grant encounter the hippopotamus-headed goddess after their supposed human death. She tells them that if their hearts prove to be balanced in life, their souls will be allowed to spend eternity in paradise, also known as the Field of Reeds. If their hearts are not balanced, their souls will be cast into the Duat, dragged down by the dead, and frozen in sand forevermore.

In order to determine their posthumous existential destiny in the Scales of Justice, Taweret simultaneously reaches into their chests and extracts crystalline versions of their hearts. Taweret places the hearts on the scales —together on one of the weighing plates since they represent a single human body. On the other, she places the Feather of Truth. The scales do not stop moving and Taweret, never having seen the scales react like this before, determines that Marc's and Steven's hearts are not full. She suggests that they dive back into their memories to find out what elements are hidden from this moment of judgment, and that they show each other the truth of their lives before the Duat claims their souls.

When it is later determined that Marc's heart is balanced and he is permitted to enter the Field of Reeds, he finds he cannot live a truly peaceful afterlife if he lets his alter Steven be cast away alone into the endless sands of Duat. Eventually, Marc renounces eternal life in the Field of Reeds to save Steven and they both return from the afterlife together.

43

Kamala Khan's Bangle

Used by: Aisha, Kamala Khan, Dar-Benn
Years in recent use: 1942 to the present day

The era of origin has not been confirmed for this handsome bangle, which is decorated with emerald-colored designs, a sun motif, and other filigree details. It was discovered by Aisha, leader of the mystical Clandestines—exiles from the Noor Dimension—in the rubble of a ruined Ten Rings temple in India in 1942. When the golden metal bracelet is worn by a descendant of the Noor Dimension, it expands and emits a purple glow. A rush of energy enhances its wearer's innate powers and enables them to time travel.

In 1947, the bangle was handed down to Sana, daughter of Aisha and an Indian rose farmer named Hasan as they were making their way to Pakistan. Sana later sent the bangle to her granddaughter, Kamala, in a package. Kamala's mother, Muneeba, believed that the items Sana had passed down to Kamala were merely junk.

When Kamala dons the artifact as part of her Captain Marvel costume for the New Jersey AvengerCon, she has a transcendental experience. She soon discovers that, when wearing the bangle, she can generate waves of energy in a crystalline form she describes as "hard light," which allows her to accomplish amazing feats, such as rescuing a classmate from a fall by catching her with a visualized hand or creating stepping stones for herself in mid-air. The bangle also enables Kamala to travel back in time to a pivotal moment in her family's history and uncover more about her great grandmother Aisha, notably her leadership role within the Clandestines.

During a later, unexpected, star-struck rendezvous with Captain Marvel and Monica Rambeau, Kamala discovers that her bangle pairs with one possessed by Kree leader Dar-Benn, and that the two bangles worn together provide immense—but temporary—power to Dar-Benn. This ultimately leads to Dar-Benn's demise and Kamala's ownership of both bangles, which are revealed to be Kree Quantum Bands.

44

Stormbreaker

Used by: Thor, Captain America, Axl Heimdallson, Gorr's daughter
Years in use: 2018 to the present day

Thor adopts Stormbreaker as a replacement for his beloved Mjolnir after Hela destroys Mjolnir and the God of Thunder needs a new weapon to fight the Titan Thanos.

Stormbreaker was designed by the Dwarves of Nidavellir to serve as the most powerful Asgardian weapon. However, the battle-ax was not completed until forged by Thor's special request in 2018. This task required the reignition of an ancient forge, which had lain dormant after Thanos raided the planet to compel the Dwarves to craft the all-powerful Infinity Gauntlet. After this task had been completed, Thanos massacred the Dwarvian population to the verge of extinction, leaving only Eitri alive.

After Eitri forges the ax, Stormbreaker's handle is manifested courtesy of Groot. Along with Rocket, he has accompanied Thor to Nidavellir and generously donates one of his his own limbs to complete the weapon.

Although Stormbreaker is extremely impressive in hand-to-hand combat—as shown by its piercing and ultimate decapitation of Thanos in 2018—the ax has proved useful in other ways. It conducts teleportation via the summoning of the Bifrost; it channels Thor's power over weather and electricity; it enables its wielder to fly; and it delivers healing energy to Thor after his exposure to the neutron star heat released by the Nidavellirian forge.

Stormbreaker is briefly used by Captain America in the Battle of Earth in 2023, and inadvertently falls into the villainous hands of Gorr the God Butcher during the battle at the Gates of Eternity in 2025, before being reclaimed by Thor. The God of Thunder then directs Axl Heimdallson to use Stormbreaker to summon the Bifrost and enable himself and other Asgardian youth to reach the safety of New Asgard. Thor later gives Stormbreaker to Gorr's daughter, whom he has adopted, to wield.

45

The Bloodstone

Used by: The Bloodstone family
Years in use: The distant past to the present day

The Bloodstone is deep garnet in color and rich in power, exhibiting capabilities that grant its keeper protection, longevity, and strength. Although its exact date of origin is unknown, the Bloodstone is depicted in an antique tapestry at Bloodstone Manor. This features knight-like individuals who, from their attire, appear to belong to the medieval era.

The Bloodstone family charts its possession of the gem back to Ulysses Bloodstone, a wealthy, renowned monster hunter in his time on Earth. A portrait shows him wearing the Bloodstone on his chest.

In the manor's magnificent main hall, decorated with monstrous trophies, mysterious antiques, and paintings depicting famous monster hunts such as George and the Dragon, the Bloodstone has pride of place. The stone is initially attached to the ornate cover of an impressive-looking tome mounted upon a tall occasional table.

The death of Ulysses Bloodstone requires his widow Verussa, in accordance with tradition, to find a successor to continue Ulysses' monster-hunting mission. Verussa summons five of the foremost hunters in the world, with 200 kills between them—Jovan, Liorn, Barasso, Azarel, and Jack Russell, plus Ulysses' daughter Elsa, who regards the Bloodstone as her birthright—to the Bloodstone estate to compete to possess the powerful stone. Verussa is particularly skeptical of Elsa's chances as, after showing great promise, she rejected her father Ulysses' training methods and became the greatest disappointment of his life.

The competition takes place in a maze in the grounds and requires the champion to conquer Ted—the creature also known as Man-Thing—who has been cruelly captured for the purpose by Verussa. The Bloodstone is chained to Ted in order to weaken him and also make him angry. Ultimately, Jack Russell—secretly Ted's friend and a werewolf—and Elsa rescue Ted, who then kills Verussa. Elsa Bloodstone becomes the keeper of the gem, and thus the Bloodstone stays within the current familial heritage.

Essential Equipment

This section explores a wide variety of objects used on secret missions by the heroes and villains of the Marvel Cinematic Universe, including high-powered vehicles, exo-suits that give their wearers remarkable powers, and a flying device that facilitates reconnaissance and surveillance. The smallest items can have the most spectacular effects: They can make people and things change size, or keep a hero's heart beating.

46

Captain America's WWII Motorbike

Used by: Steve Rogers

Years in use: The 1940s

A motorcycle is Steve Rogers' vehicle of choice both personally and as super soldier Captain America. As such it perfectly reflects Cap's adventurous free spirit. This particular model is a customized Harley-Davidson bike, crafted by the Strategic Scientific Reserve (SSR) and used by Cap during World War II missions on the battlefields of Europe. Unique features added to this model include a rear flamethrower, a tripwire function, a forward-facing explosive launcher, and an auto-pilot option, all controlled by the small keypad installed on the left side handlebar. This motorcycle also includes a gun holster attached to a frame on the right side of the front fender and a bracket on the front of the cycle designed to hold Captain America's vibranium shield in place to deflect enemy firepower.

This model serves its final call of duty when Captain America leaps off of it to embark in

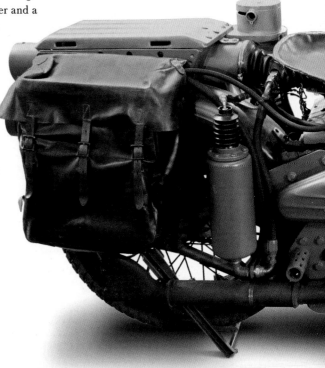

hand-to-hand combat while sending the motorcycle forward to crash and explode, opening the entryway to the Hydra headquarters for further infiltration by fellow SSR forces. A replica of this motorcycle is added to a historic exhibit on Captain America, on display for fans to enjoy and, coincidentally, for the cryogenically-preserved Steve Rogers to see some 70 years after he rode the original version.

Captain America once again rides a powerful two-wheeler into battle in Sokovia in 2015. During this anti-Hydra mission he launches his motorcycle as an explosive device toward a Hydra soldier transport.

47

Captain America's Compass

Used by: Steve Rogers
Years in use: The 1940s to the present day

This compass belongs to Steve Rogers (Captain America) and dates back to the 1940s. It also contains an image of Agent Peggy Carter, who held a Strategic Scientific Reserve post in the U.S. military when Rogers joined the Super Soldier Program's Project Rebirth in 1943.

The success of Project Rebirth led to Rogers embodying the role of Captain America and working closely on a number of challenging assignments alongside Carter. This time and experience together led to Rogers and Carter forming a close relationship—as her photo in his trusty compass attests.

Rogers employed the compass throughout his World War II career. It even survived his plunge into the freezing depths of the North Atlantic Ocean aboard the aircraft *Valkyrie* in 1945—a heroic effort to keep the heavily armed vehicle from crashing and exploding among the innocent citizens of New York. Remarkably, after Rogers is found and rejuvenated out of cryogenic stasis decades later, the compass is still intact. Rogers catches up with his own history—and is reminded of Carter's crucial place in it—at an historical exhibition in Washington, D.C. in 2014.

The compass accompanies Captain America on an important mission to bring down Thanos aboard the Guardians' spacecraft in 2018, showing that even though the instrument is not effective in outer space, it still holds great value to its owner. Multiple versions of Captain America find this object important when they fight among themselves in Stark Tower during the Time Heist of 2023.

48

Hydra's Submarine

Used by: Hydra agent Fred Clemson
Years in use: Unknown to 1943

This mini sub is waiting to pick up a Hydra agent, who introduces himself as Fred Clemson from the State Department, after he assassinates Dr. Abraham Erskine and seizes a sample of his Super Soldier Serum. Clemson is among a party of dignitaries gathered in Erskine's Strategic Scientific Reserve lab to witness the breakthrough process by which Steve Rogers will become the U.S. Army's first super soldier.

Erskine administers the final infusion of serum, and Rogers is enclosed in a metal capsule while he receives the necessarily high dose of Vita Rays

to complete the procedure. He suffers immense pain, but emerges alive and physically enhanced. As the high-ranking spectators gather to congratulate Erskine, Clemson explodes a bomb in the viewing gallery, steals a vial of serum, and shoots Dr. Erskine dead before fleeing.

Agent Carter fires and wounds Clemson, and Steve Rogers, now the U.S.'s only super soldier, pursues on foot as Clemson leaps into a taxi cab. The high-speed, bullet-riddled chase ends at Brooklyn's Pier 13 and reverts into a foot race. Hopelessly outmatched, Clemson takes a boy hostage in order to make Rogers stand down, then ruthlessly tosses him into the waters of the harbor. Rogers is momentarily nonplussed, but the boy bravely tells him "I can swim." Clemson runs along the pier as the Hydra submarine rises from the depths, revealing itself to be a sleek black boat with dual engines that flank a single-person cockpit.

Clemson leaps into the pilot's seat and the sub begins to submerge. Rogers dives into the water, punches through the sub's windshield, and rips Clemson out of the craft. Rogers tosses him ashore, but the stolen Super Soldier Serum vial smashes on the ground, spilling its precious contents. Issuing a final "Hail Hydra" statement of allegiance, Clemson takes his own life with a cyanide capsule. Hydra's damaged submarine sinks to the bottom of New York Harbor, and Steve Rogers—soon to be dubbed a "Nazi-fighting Mystery Man" in the press—has achieved the first of his many victories against the malign forces of Hydra.

49

Nick Fury's S.H.I.E.L.D. Pass

Used by: Nick Fury
Year in use: 1995

This is an official ID pass for Nicholas Joseph Fury, agent of the Strategic Homeland Intervention, Enforcement and Logistics Division (S.H.I.E.L.D.), the U.S. governmental organization focused on countering threats from any source that challenges national and global security. This pass dates from 1995, years before Fury became S.H.I.E.L.D.S.'s director—as the security clearance level "03" indicates. At this time, he and Agent Phil Coulson encounter Vers, formerly U.S. Air Force pilot Carol Danvers, who has gained special powers after being exposed to the Tesseract. She alerts Fury that shape-shifting extraterrestrials the Skrulls are set to invade Earth. It turns out that the Kree—the Skrulls' bitter enemies—are more of a threat. By the time the situation is resolved, Fury has lost an eye, after a too-close encounter with another alien, a Flerken, which has swallowed the Tesseract and has the appearance of a domestic cat.

His missing eye covered by an eye patch, Fury, now S.H.I.E.L.D.'s director, creates the Avengers Initiative in 2012. This utilizes the collective power of heroic enhanced beings in order to protect the U.S. and the planet from predicaments often involving extraterrestrial forces. The Avengers' first mission is to defeat Loki, who has stolen the Tesseract and is leading an invasion of Earth by the Chitauri. The Avengers Initiative proves to be a powerful resource in this instance, but is brought into question in 2016 when great damage is wrought in Lagos, Nigeria, and innocent lives are lost during a mission to thwart Hydra operatives.

Fury is so dedicated to his work that when S.H.I.E.L.D. is infiltrated by Hydra agents in 2014, he fakes his own death in order to fight the good fight undercover. He is one of the individuals who disappears in Thanos' Snap of 2018; restored five years later, he continues to work with the Avengers, and particularly Captain Marvel, from an intergalactic space station and the S.A.B.E.R. organization.

50

Arc Reactor

Used by: Howard Stark, Tony Stark, Obadiah Stane
Years in use: The 1960s to 2023

This small device is best known for powering Iron Man armor in the early 2000s. However, the origins of this amazing technology date back many decades earlier.

In the 1940s, Howard Stark discovers the vast energies contained in an ancient artifact named the Tesseract, which Hydra has tried to exploit for military purposes. Recovering the Tesseract from the depths of the North Atlantic Ocean, Stark hopes to create a sustainable, non-nuclear energy source that the entire planet can utilize and not have to fight over in future worldwide wars. With Russian scientist Anton Vanko, a defector to the U.S. in 1963, Stark develops an early form of Arc Reactor. However, Stark Industries does not have the resources or technology to take their discoveries to the next level; instead, an early form of Arc Reactor is used to create high-tech weaponry for the U.S. military.

Arc Reactor research is relaunched in 2008 by next-generation inventor Tony Stark while captured by The Ten Rings criminal organization in Afghanistan. An ingenious, miniaturized version of the giant reactor powering Stark industries, Tony's Arc Reactor is designed to keep his heart—injured in a bomb explosion—from ceasing to beat. This Arc Reactor not only helps keep Tony alive; it also becomes the power source for the first-ever Iron Man armor, devised by Tony and fellow captive Dr. Ho Yinsen, that enables him to escape The Ten Rings' compound.

Back in the U.S., Tony develops an improved version of his Arc Reactor and gives the original to Pepper Potts. She has it engraved with a humorous motto and preserved in a glass case. Obadiah Stane steals Tony's new Arc Reactor, and Tony uses the one Pepper fortunately kept to defeat him.

Following the Time Heist of 2023, the grieving Pepper makes Tony's original Arc Reactor the centerpiece of a floral wreath at his funeral.

51

Holo-Map Projector

Used by: Star-Lord
Year in use: 2014

This device is a combination of historical record and 3D navigation system. Peter Quill, also known as Star-Lord, makes use of this holo-map projector to find a valuable object known as the Orb for the Broker in 2014. Seeking to win the bounty for himself, he opts to go rogue from the Ravagers gang of space bandits, who abducted him from Earth as a child and raised him.

After landing on the planet Morag, Quill turns on the device and its blue beam casts a laser-outlined framework of structures upon an otherwise desolate landscape. The device also projects activities of individuals in the virtual space, conveying a sense of liveliness that is not apparent in the real-world environment. Despite the dark, rocky, and rainy conditions, Quill makes his way through the mapped-out space with a beat in his step, thanks to the soundtrack on his beloved cassette player, making an otherwise difficult journey more like a dance party.

The holo-map projector eventually shows him the way into temple ruins, whereupon he discovers the Orb. Quill takes possession of it but does not have an easy return back to his ship because Korath, a cybernetic Kree soldier, is also on a mission to collect the Orb—which contains the Power Stone—at the behest of Kree warlord Ronan. Quill eventually evades Korath and his brigade and flies away from Morag, only to encounter further complications with the Orb when he tries to deliver it to the Broker on Xandar, who doesn't want anything to do with the artifact when he learns that Ronan covets it.

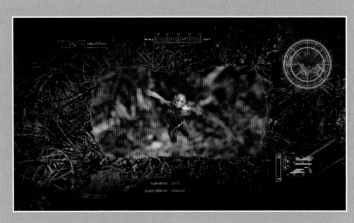

There is no hiding place for Ant-Man when Falcon uses his goggles' thermal-imaging function.

52

Falcon's Goggles

Used by: Sam Wilson
Years in use: 2015 to 2024

These high-tech goggles are a key component to the Falcon uniform, an exosuit worn by Sam Wilson when he is on Avengers missions. They not only protect Wilson's eyes while he is in flight, they also offer advanced features such as thermal imaging capabilities powerful enough to detect the tiniest living objects, for example a greatly reduced Ant-Man.

A screen display inside the goggles allows Falcon to view the thermal image and can also show an enhanced, zoomed-in visual of the target, alongside other diagnostic information that enables Falcon to home in on his quarry. The goggles also help Falcon to track a moving target in a crowded space.

The goggles serve as a vital connection to Falcon's Redwing accessory, the remote-controlled drone housed on Falcon's back until it is launched to operate independently. Using the goggles' interior display, Falcon can view the area over which Redwing flies via its front-housed camera, considerably increasing his surveillance range and abilities. Redwing's scanner also conveys vital tactical information to Falcon through his goggles, such as the explosive contents of a dumpster commandeered as a battering ram by enemies led by Crossbones in Lagos in 2016. By way of this scanner-goggles link, Falcon detects Crossbones stealing a bio-weapon on the third floor of the Institute of Infectious Diseases.

Whether the Falcon uniform is an earlier model constructed with Stark technology or a later version enhanced with vibranium courtesy of the Wakandan scientific team, the goggles remain an essential part of Sam Wilson's mission equipment. He incorporates them with his Captain America suit when he takes on that mantle in 2023.

53

Pym Particle Discs

Used by: Hank Pym, Hope Van Dyne, Scott Lang
Years in use: Unknown to the present day

These small objects are remarkable technological devices developed by Dr. Hank Pym to serve as a vital part of Ant-Man's equipment. When thrown, they instigate rapid size manipulation of any target.

The red disc shrinks objects and the blue disc enlarges them, courtesy of innovative quantum energy science honed by Pym and channeled into a substance he calls Pym Particles. These particles change the distance between atoms, affecting the density and strength of the item with which they come into contact. The discs are stored in a compartment on Ant-Man's suit belt and are easily dispensed by Ant-Man and his ally Hope Van Dyne, a.k.a. The Wasp, at any size and at any given moment, allowing them to dramatically alter the size of obstacles, vehicles, enemies, allies, and more, and delivering a jarring element of surprise to adversaries.

In 2015, Scott Lang uses a red disc to shrink his deadly opponent Yellowjacket when the villain invades his ex-wife's home and threatens their daughter, Cassie. In the same battle, he uses a blue disc to massively increase the size of one of his own ant teammates to help protect Cassie.

When dealing with inanimate objects, Ant-Man uses a blue disc to enlarge a tank truck that Captain America hurls during the battle among the Avengers' ranks at Leipzig-Halle Airport in 2016, and The Wasp uses another to massively enlarge a plastic candy dispenser she throws at an enemy motorbike rider during a high-speed chase through the streets of San Francisco in 2018.

54

Redwing

Used by: Falcon

Years in use: 2015 to the present day

This multi-functional drone unit was developed at Stark Labs, the first of several Redwing models that have been crafted for Avengers' work. Redwing is carried on the back of the armor of the Falcon, a.k.a. Sam Wilson, a former U.S. Air Force pararescue officer. Redwing is controlled by Falcon's voice and digital commands to execute tasks that involve combat, accessibility, and surveillance.

Redwing has a variety of built-in weaponry including twin guns, a stun missile, and a grappling line. Its power is considerable, as Spider-Man and Iron Man discover during a battle at Leipzig-Halle Airport in 2016. Its compact, hawk-like presence also provides superb remote reconnaissance support. The drone makes its mark during a 2016 battle in Lagos, Nigeria, during an attack led by Crossbones (Brock Rumlow) on the Institute for Infectious Diseases (IFID). While in flight, the unit analyzes a garbage truck by flying beneath the vehicle as it thunders toward the IFID. Using Redwing's X-ray abilities, Falcon realizes that the truck is a battering ram clearing the way for enemy vehicles to follow through the broken security gate. Redwing then scans the building to discover Crossbones' location, and later fires on an operative confronting Black Widow.

During a battle with Thanos in Wakanda in 2018, Redwing displays thrice-impressive prowess. An upgrade by a local engineering team enables the drone to break into three pieces and pierce Thanos' minions with the force of sheer speed in flight. This work on Redwing gives Wakandan engineers a path to develop an even better version of the drone for Falcon after his reappearance when the Blip ends in 2023.

Redwing proves to be an effective tool at high altitude as well, as shown in a mission to rescue Captain Vassant, captured by Georges Batroc and his LAF group in 2024. Using its pulse-laser cutting feature, Redwing slices open the side of an aircraft in mid-air to allow Falcon to enter, then proceeds to blow up an LAF helicopter to keep it off Falcon's tail.

55

Taskmaster Suit

Used by: Antonia Dreykov
Year in use: 2016

This battle suit is worn by Taskmaster, a fighting persona embodied by Antonia Dreykov, the most highly developed special agent produced through the Red Room initiative under the direction of her father, General Dreykov. The Red Room is an underground operation that abducts young girls, trains them in combat and espionage techniques, and keeps them under chemical subjugation to serve as international human weapons known as Widows. In her youth, Antonia suffers great physical distress from an explosion that Natasha Romanoff, a Widow trainee herself, instigates, intending to kill Dreykov and put a stop to his abhorrent program. Unbeknownst to Romanoff, her assassination attempt fails, and Dreykov takes this opportunity to turn his damaged daughter into his greatest weapon yet, naming her Taskmaster.

Taskmaster has been trained to mimic the most iconic and effective fighting talents of the Avengers. For example, she can wield a shield as handily as Captain America, using it to deflect bullets, as a projectile to hurl at targets, and also as a blunt-force weapon. She can engage in hand-to-hand combat as effectively as the Winter Soldier; metallic claws similar to Black Panther's spring from her gloved fingers; and she can fire an explosive arrow with the accuracy of Hawkeye.

Taskmaster's helmet has built-in tactical capabilities that assess a foe, revealing identity and threat levels while also helping her calculate possible defensive measures to be utilized in battle. Finally, perhaps Taskmaster's most compelling talent is her ability to mirror and match the martial arts combat moves of Black Widow. Antonia is not freed from her deadly Taskmaster persona until Black Widow exposes her to the antidote to General Dreykov's cruel mind control.

56

Black Panther Suit

Used by: T'Chaka, T'Challa, N'Jadaka, Shuri
Years in use: Unknown to the present day

The Black Panther suit is the uniform of a highly revered icon in Wakandan culture, and is also respected worldwide when associated with the Avengers. For generations, the mantle of Black Panther, protector of Wakanda, aligned with whoever was Ruler of Wakanda, with T'Chaka preceding his son T'Challa, and N'Jadaka succeeding his cousin T'Challa after a challenge for the crown. When Shuri is called to be the next Black Panther, however, she does not simultaneously seek the crown.

The Black Panther suit is effectively a battle suit worn by an individual who has consumed the Heart-Shaped Herb that grants the Black Panther physical protection and power. After the essence of its flower is ingested, the herb mentally transports the Black Panther to the Ancestral Plane and grants him or her superhuman strength, speed, and perception.

The Black Panther suit is sleek, and the Wakandan Design Group provides ever-evolving versions. T'Challa receives an upgrade to his suit when Shuri, the leader of the Design Group while he is king, presents him with a new model that is stored within the teeth design of a necklace, primed to engage the full suit when the Black Panther requires. The necklace receives a message transmitted from T'Challa's synched vibranium implant and then proceeds to materialize the suit with his mental command.

Each model of the suit is woven with fiber made of vibranium, the strongest substance in the universe according to Wakandan legend, found only in the Wakandan and Talokanil regions of the world after a meteor crash millions of years prior directly impacted those environments. The vibranium weave makes T'Challa's suit strong, flexible, and protective, while an upgraded version also contains nanites. These are able to absorb kinetic energy that hits the suit, allowing the Black Panther to release said energy when needed in battle.

When T'Challa is outnumbered and repeatedly struck by Killmonger's army of Border Tribe warriors, his suit glows as it stores their weapons' energy. Black Panther then suddenly releases a purple-hued force field that hurls them aside.

T'Challa's Black Panther helmet
is laid to rest when he passes to
the Ancestral Realm.

The suit is also bulletproof and even capable of repelling Hawkeye's explosive arrows, taking and withstanding hits from them at close range during the battle between the Avengers at Leipzig-Halle Airport in 2016.

The nanite structure of the newer models of the Black Panther suit offers regeneration capabilities, should some weapon manage to penetrate the suit. T'Challa's model repairs itself after taking an energy hit from Ulysses Klaue, and Shuri's suit displays regeneration capabilities when she is speared by Namor, who also uses a vibranium weapon—a greater challenge to her than the more conventional weapons employed against Black Panthers in the past.

The Black Panther suit features retractable vibranium claws on both gauntlets. These claws can be deployed for increased grip or to slash opponents during hand-to-hand combat. They are incredibly strong and sharp weapons, even capable of inflicting deep scratches on Captain America's vibranium shield when T'Challa and Black Panther come into conflict during the airport clash. On another occasion, T'Challa uses his claws to grip onto the top of a car driving at high speed through Busan, South Korea.

Subsequently, Shuri uses her claws to gain purchase on the superstructure of the Wakandan *Sea Leopard* as she helps the Dora Milaje repel Talokanil warriors. Shuri also shows her claws when facing Namor and his spear. In addition, Shuri's gauntlets contain hidden ship controls and can fire powerful concussive blasts of energy.

Another notable element of the Black Panther suit is its helmet. In earlier versions, this is placed on Black Panther's head but later upgrades enable the helmet to materialize on the mental command of its wearer. The design of the helmet varies from model to model; T'Chaka, T'Challa, N'Jadaka, and Shuri— who designs her own helmet— each sport unique versions during their time as Black Panther that reflect their individual styles.

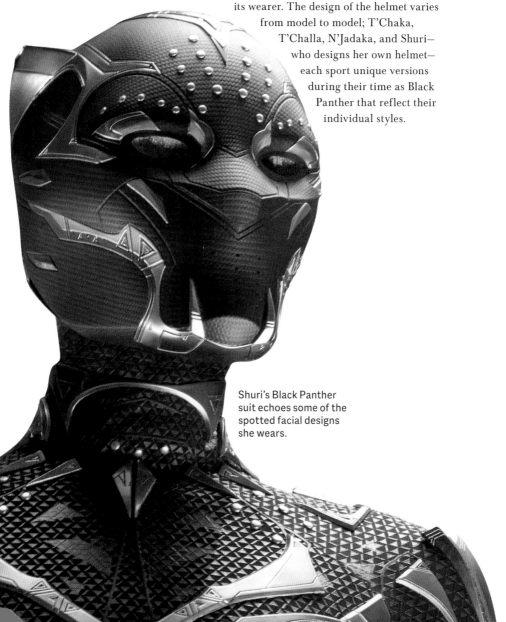

Shuri's Black Panther suit echoes some of the spotted facial designs she wears.

57

N'Jadaka's Black Panther Suit

Used by: Erik "Killmonger" Stevens, a.k.a. N'Jadaka
Year in use: 2016

When N'Jadaka wins the crown of Wakanda and the honor of serving as Black Panther from his cousin T'Challa, he portrays his new lofty role in a very different manner and look. Whereas T'Challa had chosen to wear an understated necklace, N'Jadaka selects a more ostentatious golden option from which his Black Panther suit materializes. When not suited up as the Black Panther, N'Jadaka tends to wear the necklace over his bare chest, framed by a cloak, and boldly showing the markings of his kill count emblazoned on his skin.

The Black Panther suit worn by N'Jadaka is one of the newer models that the Wakandan Design Group has created. When fully materialized, the suit features a great deal of golden detail which on the helmet resembles the markings of a leopard. When the suit absorbs energy, it glows with an orange tint as opposed to the purple aura that T'Challa's suit exhibits. N'Jadaka's suit possesses remarkable regeneration capabilities should some weapon attempt to penetrate it: when Shuri blasts energy from her gauntlets at him, the nanites in his Black Panther suit appear to dissipate momentarily before they shift back together to seal up the gap created. When T'Challa and the new Black Panther, N'Jadaka, battle one another, both of their suits exhibit the shifting of nanites. T'Challa's knowledge of this characteristic and how to exploit a momentary weakness of his opponent's suit enables him to defeat N'Jadaka and regain his place as the King of Wakanda.

58

The Mighty Thor's Armor

Used by: Jane Foster
Year in use: 2025

Dr. Jane Foster is a renowned astrophysicist whose work takes her to New Mexico in 2010 to study an astronomical anomaly. Foster later realizes that the anomaly correlates to Thor's banishment from Asgard, which has landed him and Mjolnir on Earth. After hearing Thor's story, Foster's fascination with the greater universe grows and she comes to understand it on an even deeper level. Foster and Thor fall in love, but the two face challenges as residents of different worlds—one an ordinary human being and the other a near-immortal god. In addition, Jane becomes more and more involved with her research and writing, while the action-loving Thor safeguards Earth as one of the Avengers.

In 2013, Foster is studying gravitational anomalies—indicative of a Convergence of the Nine Realms—in London, and is suddenly sucked into a wormhole that pulls her into proximity with the Aether, which infiltrates her body. She thus becomes a prime target for the leader of the Dark Elves, Malekith, who subsequently extracts it from her for his own nefarious uses.

Foster is one of the unfortunate persons who disappear in the Titan Thanos' Snap in 2018, and upon her return in 2023 she is afflicted with cancer, reaching stage 4 by 2025. When she and Thor were dating, Thor had asked Mjolnir to always protect Jane. She is drawn to visit the remnants of the now-shattered Mjolnir, which is preserved in a glass case in New Asgard, hoping that it might help cure her. Instead, her presence completely restores the hammer, which chooses her as its worthy wielder.

Mjolnir transforms Foster into the superhuman Mighty Thor, outfitted with suitably heroic armor. The Mighty Thor battles alongside Thor to save the children of New Asgard from a horrible fate envisioned by Gorr the God Butcher. The star-crossed lovers' joy is short-lived, however, as the use of Mjolnir and the strenuous effort of battle proves too much for Foster's cancer-ridden body.

59

Talokanil Rebreather

Used by: Talokanil warriors
Years in use: 2025

This mask-like device is a piece of Talokanil technology that enables those who live underwater to breathe when in air. K'uk'ulkan, leader of the Talokanil people but known by his enemies as Namor, is furious that his culture's invaluable vibranium has been discovered by outsiders who wish to mine it. He approaches the leaders of Wakanda to seek their support in protecting their precious resource, no matter what the cost. When he does not get the agreement he seeks, he proceeds to launch an attack upon Shuri and the American creator of a vibranium detector with whom she has connected, college student Riri Williams. This attack requires a squad of his water-sustained warriors to come up onto land, relying on their respirators to function.

Talokanil forces abduct Shuri and Williams on a bridge over Boston's Charles River, despite Okoye's brave attempts to fight them off. Namor hopes to extract an agreement for them to work together to protect their homelands from further intrusion by those outside of the Wakandan and Talokanil cultures.

Namor's hopes are dashed when Nakia comes to the rescue of Shuri and Williams. Declaring war, his forces flood Wakanda and succeed in drowning Queen Ramonda. A full-scale battle with Wakandan forces ensues, requiring all Talokanil individuals to wear respirators in air or land-based clashes.

After much blood has been spilt, Shuri and Namor find a compromise and forge a peaceful path forward together.

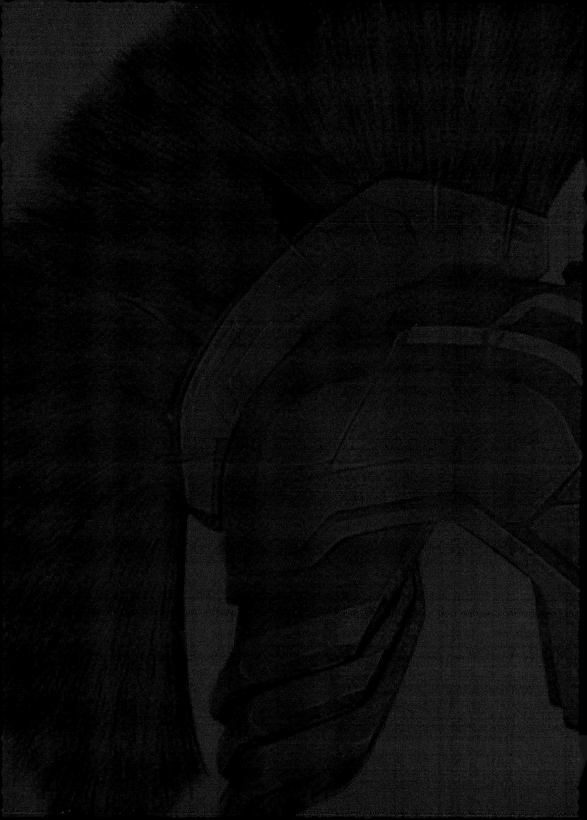

Battle Ready

Featured in this selection are artifacts honed into various styles of intriguing weaponry that uniquely reflect the individual or forces that carry them into battle. Some—like Captain America's vibranium shield—project an iconic sense of heroism. Others—like Ronan's hammer—instill terror. But whether serving offensive, defensive, or protective purposes, these weapons have impacted many of the most unforgettable clashes in MCU history.

60

Captain America's WW II Suit

Used by: Steve Rogers
Years in use: 1943 to 1945

When Steve Rogers agrees to serve in the Army as Captain America his earliest days are more for show than for battle, with Rogers making personal appearances as part of lavish theatrical productions meant to pump up war bond sales and recruitment for the U.S. military. Rogers longs to make a more important contribution to winning the war and, with Agent Carter's help, embarks on a renegade solo mission to rescue a battalion of captured soldiers from the 107th Infantry Regiment—including his friend Bucky Barnes—from an Austrian Hydra weapons facility. To do so, he adds a leather jacket to his theatrical costume along with goggles and his prop metal heater shield. Well aware that he needs a helmet to face the foe, he exchanges the cloth winged mask he wears in his stage act for one of the chorus girls' prop helmets. The helmet features a bold "A" for America emblazoned on the front and a wing motif.

Agent Carter arranges for a transport plane, piloted by Howard Stark, to parachute Captain America to the vicinity of the Hydra facility, 30 miles behind enemy lines. As anti-aircraft shells explode around the plane, Cap bravely parachutes out. Infiltrating the Hydra weapons factory, he then locates and rescues the soldiers who have been forced to work building Hydra's Tesseract-empowered weapons. Freed, the infantrymen seize Hydra's own high-tech weaponry and attack their captors.

Hydra's leader, Johann von Schmidt, a.k.a. the Red Skull, gets his first look at Captain America in full flow via a closed-circuit surveillance monitor. Quickly realizing his forces are outmatched, he decides to blow up the factory and escape. As it explodes, Cap finds and rescues Bucky and then leads the brave men of the 107th back to camp in triumph.

After the resounding success of this mission, Captain America is granted official battle duties, fulfilling his ambition to stand with troops on the battlefield instead of showgirls on the stage. Rogers sets to work with inventor Howard Stark of the Strategic Scientific Reserve to come up with

Years later, Captain America's
outfit and shield are put
on display as part of an
exhibition celebrating his
heroic World War II exploits.

a military-grade Captain America uniform and proper accessories.
Captain America's improved outfit represents a rugged form of patriotism
from head to toe, adorned in red-white-and-blue glory but with a practical,
utilitarian emphasis. The bodysuit is carbon polymer—tough enough to
withstand a bayonet thrust, according to Stark—with leather straps, durable
metal fasteners and muscular body-contouring accents. The overall effect is
a striking addition to Cap's commanding battlefield presence. His garb is
completed by a sturdy utility belt and gun holster as well as thick leather
gloves and boots. The gloves are particularly handy when managing Cap's
new and improved vibranium shield—another cutting-edge Stark product.

Captain America's reformatted All-American hero continues to be a
daunting figure throughout World War II, scoring victory after victory.
He and his team of Howling Commandos—comprising Bucky and several of
the battle-hardened men from the 107th that Cap had previously rescued—
traverse Western Europe seeking out and destroying Hydra bases. One of

their most successful missions turns out to be traumatic for Captain America. During the Howling Commandos' capture of lead Hydra scientist Doctor Arnim Zola on a train in the Alps, his best friend Bucky Barnes seemingly falls to his death.

Although future Captain America uniforms are modernized according to the latest military technology and innovative materials available, they continue to honor the spirit first woven into the Captain American persona.

No longer a stage prop, Captain America's World War II helmet shows it's battle scars.

61

Captain America's Shield

Used by: Steve Rogers, Sam Wilson, John Walker
Years in use: 1943 to the present day

Captain America's red-white-and-blue shield became a key element of his persona shortly after he underwent his transformation into the U.S.'s sole super soldier in June 1943. Initially, Cap's shield was more of a stage show prop than a weapon. Crafted in a medieval, heater style, his original shield served as a convenient holder of hidden cue cards from which Steve Rogers read during his wartime traveling performances across the nation selling war bonds and gaining recruits for the military. However, his heater shield subsequently proved worthy of seeing battle action; Rogers took it with him when he set out to rescue a large group of captured soldiers—including his childhood friend Bucky Barnes—from a Hydra base. The success of this mission helped convince the Army that Captain America could be more useful as an active soldier than as a glorified bond salesman.

The development of Captain America's iconic circular shield dates back to 1943, when Steve Rogers is drawn to a prototype in Howard Stark's Strategic Scientific Reserve development laboratory. A round, silver-colored circular object shelved under a worktable catches Rogers' eye. After hearing from Stark that this disc is made of vibranium and "stronger than steel, a third of the weight, and completely vibration absorbent," Rogers is even more intrigued by its potential. Agent Carter pumps a fusillade of bullets at it, shocking the entire weapons development laboratory but clearly demonstrating the vibranium's strength. Stark then refines the prototype shield to reflect the look of Captain America's suit.

The new circular shield is put to the test in the field when Captain America and his Howling Commandos power across Western Europe on a mission to shut down Hydra bases and specifically the work of Hydra's chief scientific officer Johann Schmidt, the Red Skull. This blaze of glory spans 1943 through 1945 and then abruptly ends when Captain America makes the difficult, self-sacrificing decision to crash-land the *Valkyrie*, a Hydra aircraft loaded with Tesseract-powered bombs, into the Arctic Ocean instead of allowing it to devastate a populated area of the U.S. With that

Cap's original World War II heater-style shield.

heroic act, both Captain America and his iconic shield are frozen in icy waters for nearly 70 years.

After the plane is found and Steve Rogers is awakened and acclimated to the new world conditions, the latest director of S.H.I.E.L.D., Nick Fury, reestablishes the role of Captain America and sets Rogers up with a modernized version of his uniform, including a refresh of his shield. In 2012, his shield has its first otherworldly test when it withstands Chitauri energy blasts. Captain America has used the shield not only to deflect projectiles and blows—even from Thor's hammer Mjolnir—when it is hand-held; but he has also benefited from its protection when it is strapped on his back or mounted on the front of his motorcycle. He has also regularly used his shield as a projectile in the midst of battle, tossing it with great power and accuracy on a trajectory that allows it to return to his hands after striking its intended target. Captain America and his shield seem inseparable up until a moment of great turmoil among the Avengers, when Iron Man tells Cap that he is not worthy of the shield his father Howard made for him. Rogers drops the shield and walks away from it. Tony Stark takes possession of the iconic object, but later returns it to Captain America when the Avengers reassemble in an attempt to halt Thanos' mission to collect all the Infinity Stones. This great battle presents the only instance in which Captain America's shield comes up against an insurmountable attack, as Thanos' sword shatters the presumed unbreakable object.

Following Thanos' defeat and the reversal of the Snap, Rogers gifts his shield to Sam Wilson, who arranges for the iconic artifact to be placed in a museum exhibit celebrating Captain America. It is not on show for long —the U.S. government revives the code name and makes special ops soldier John Walker the new Captain America. When Walker discredits the role by using the shield to kill a Flag Smasher anti-nationalist, Sam Wilson finally accepts the responsibility of becoming Captain America, shield and all.

Pieces of Cap's shield— broken by Thanos' sword.

62

Hawkeye's Bow

Used by: Clint Barton, Kate Bishop
Years in use: Unknown to the present day

Clint Barton is an Agent of S.H.I.E.L.D. turned Avenger whose most remarkable talent is his archery skills. S.H.I.E.L.D. calls on Barton and his bow for a variety of missions, including heading to Budapest to assassinate Natasha Romanoff in the early 2000s and watching over the crash site of Mjolnir in 2010—which he does from a bird's-eye view appropriate for the man who would later become the Avengers hero Hawkeye.

A vital component of Barton's marksmanship is his recurve bow, which he holds in his right hand while taking aim with his arrow of choice in his left. While the model he uses varies over the course of his crime-fighting career, Barton wields his bow as if it were an extension of his body, snapping the collapsible weapon into battle-ready mode at a moment's notice. He is seemingly even able to fire an arrow without looking—as he demonstrates when the Chitauri descend upon New York City in 2012 alongside Loki in his quest to obtain the Tesseract for Thanos. Barton posts himself among the skyscraper skyline, picking off warriors and ships with ease, occasionally firing behind his back with perfect aim.

Suitably impressed is young onlooker Kate Bishop, who witnesses Barton firing arrows left and right and using his bow to fire a grappling hook onto the side of a building, enabling him to swing on it after leaping off a rooftop. She is so inspired by Barton's brave bow-wielding that, at her father's funeral, she tells her mother that she wants to protect them from future harm and that she needs a bow and arrow to do so. Flash forward to young adult Kate, who ends up fighting the Tracksuit Mafia alongside her hero Hawkeye, using his bow as they embark on a chaotic car chase through the New York City streets.

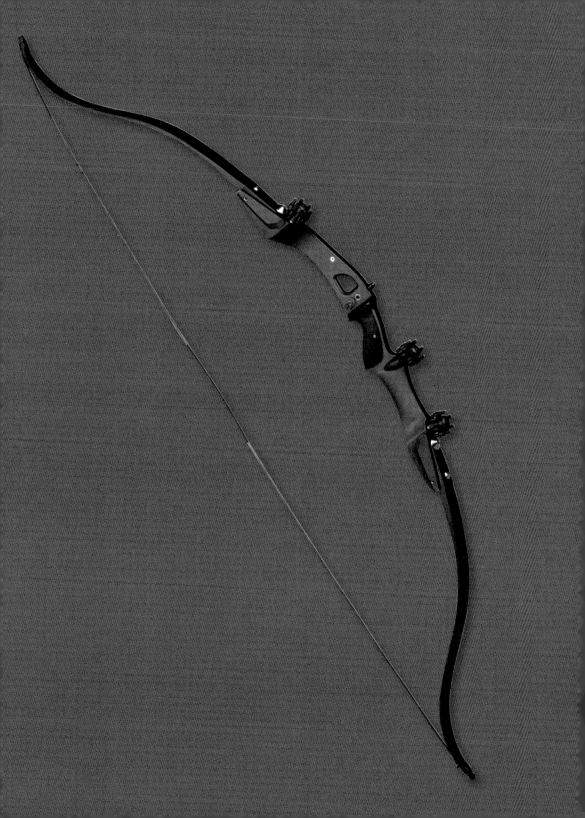

63

Chitauri Infantry Cannon

Used by: Chitauri warriors, Benjamin Pollack and Claire Weiss, S.H.I.E.L.D.
Years in use: Unknown to the present day

When the Chitauri burst into New York City at the bidding of Thanos and led by Loki in 2012, the hive-minded cyberbeings bring with them advanced alien weaponry such as this cannon. As Loki aims to steal the Tesseract in the midst of the invasion chaos, Nick Fury launches the Avengers Initiative, whereby Captain America, Black Widow, Thor, the Hulk, Iron Man, and Hawkeye mobilize as a team for the first time.

A ferocious battle ensues, culminating in victory for the Avengers and the destruction of the Chitauri once Iron Man succeeds in directing a missile to blow up their mothership—the brain source for the extraterrestrial invaders.

In the wake of the invasion, wreckage and debris cover the New York City streets, and black-market operators such as Adrian Toomes, a.k.a. the Vulture, seek abandoned alien technology in the rubble, despite the efforts of the government's Department of Damage Control, whose purpose is to collect all extraterrestrial detritus. Some highly dangerous weaponry is scavenged by Toomes and his associates, such as Jackson Brice, and enters the criminal underworld.

This particular weapon, which has the power to launch automobiles into mid-air and explode concrete structures with a single energy blast, is found by a young couple, Benjamin Pollack and Claire Weiss, who use it to rob banks. Their actions catch the attention of S.H.I.E.L.D. agents Felix Blake and Jasper Sitwell, who set out to apprehend the couple but are instead intrigued by the couple's skill with the cannon and recruit them to work with S.H.I.E.L.D. The weapon becomes cataloged as "Item 47" in the S.H.I.E.L.D. inventory, and Pollack helps the agency adapt the Chitaurian technology into artillery to be used by the military.

64

Star-Lord's Quadblaster

Used by: Peter Quill

Years in use: Unknown to the present day

Peter Quill, a.k.a. Star-Lord, is the son of human Meredith Quill and the Celestial Ego. After his mother's death, eight-year-old Peter is kidnapped from his Missouri home by space pirates the Ravagers, who become his new adoptive family. Instead of turning over the lonely young boy to his Celestial father as Ravagers' leader Yondu Udonta is meant to do, the bounty hunter takes pity on the young boy and raises him among his pirate crew, treating him like his own son. During one of their early Christmases together, Udonta shows his softer side and gifts Peter a pair of dual-barreled quadblasters, much to the boy's delight.

These blasters are nestled in holsters on Star-Lord's hips for a great majority of his time as an outlaw and/or Guardian of the Galaxy, ready for a quick draw against an opponent. The quadblasters fire a powerful blast of yellow energy to knock down a target or launch a blue taser electrical field to temporarily immobilize an opponent creature. Gamora experiences both effects when she and Quill encounter one another on Xandar, before the pair realize they are meant to be friends instead of foes.

The quadblasters prove reliable and powerful weapons on several occasions, such as when breaking out of the Kyln prison and coming to Rocket's defense when Rocket seeks to take down the High Evolutionary, who has tortured many innocent creatures in his quest for perfection. Quill's trusty quadblasters only fail him on one occasion. When trying to rescue Gamora from the clutches of Thanos during the Titan's quest to gather all the Infinity Stones, he discovers that his quadblasters will only fire harmless bubbles, owing to Thanos' possession of the Reality Stone.

65

Star-Lord's Energy Restraints

Used by: Peter Quill

Years in use: Unknown to the present day

This oval, bolas-like gadget is one of Star-Lord Peter Quill's numerous pieces of equipment. His energy restraints come in handy when a target is on the run. Quill activates the device in a split second, and throws it at his fleeing opponent. As the projectile hits its target, the object opens to release an illuminated stretch of cording that wraps itself around the target's legs, lassoing them, and dropping them to the ground.

Gamora—Thanos' adopted daughter—experiences the effectiveness of Star-Lord's energy restraints first-hand on Xandar in 2014. Because she claims to be familiar with Xandar, she is chosen by the Xandarians' fanatical enemy Ronan to obtain the Orb—which contains the Power Stone—for the Titan Thanos, who in return has promised to help Ronan destroy Xandar.

When Quill fails to sell the Orb to the Broker, who is terrified to hear that Ronan is also seeking it, Gamora engages Quill in conversation. Tossing the Orb casually in the air, he complains that the Broker has backed out of a deal with him to buy the Orb. "If there's one thing I hate, it's a man without integrity," he says. Gamora flatteringly replies that Quill has the bearing of a man of honor. She then snatches the Orb, delivers a powerful kick to Quill's midsection, and takes off, pushing bystanders aside. In a trice, Quill hurls his energy restraints device. It tangles her legs and brings her crashing to the ground. Quill catches up with her as she frees herself and the two trade blows. Before Gamora can dispatch Quill with her sword, they are both seized by bounty hunters Groot and Rocket, who are looking to earn a 40,000-unit bounty that Ravager leader Yondu Udonta has placed on Quill for stealing the Orb in the first place.

66

Rocket's Laser Gun

Used by: Rocket

Years in use: Unknown to the present day

This powerful weapon is the pride and joy of a creature barely bigger than the weapon itself, namely Rocket. Ever angry at being referred to as "vermin" (by Drax) or "a raccoon" and a "trash panda" (by Star-Lord), Rocket is a cybernetically enhanced creature, subjected to cruel experimentation by the High Evolutionary, who names him 89P13. Although the end result of the various procedures 89P13 endures turns the self-named Rocket into an engineering genius, he is profoundly bitter about his unwanted scientific journey. As a result, Rocket hates authority and

masks his better nature behind sarcasm and insults. He is also fascinated by weapons that can channel his negative energy into action, with his laser gun being a special favorite.

Before Peter Quill becomes a fellow Guardian of the Galaxy alongside Rocket, he is the target of a 40,000-unit bounty that Rocket and his partner Groot are keen to collect. During that pursuit on Xandar, Rocket takes aim at Quill with his laser gun, firing a taser shot of blue energy to bring him down. Although this chase lands Rocket, Groot, Quill, and Gamora in the Kyln, it also ultimately puts Rocket on the positive and productive path to saving Xandar from destruction by the Kree, and the formation of the Guardians of the Galaxy.

During the Avengers' ultimate war against Thanos, Rocket takes his fighting skills to a new level. He bravely engages his laser gun and other tactics in Wakanda with Black Panther, Captain America, Winter Soldier, Groot, and others as they try to fend off Thanos' Infinity Gauntlet Snap.

Along the journey of using his battle knowhow on the side of justice instead of crime, Rocket once more uses his laser gun, as part of an ambitious bid for revenge on the High Evolutionary. This culminates in victory as he and his fellow Guardians help past, present, and potential future lab subjects break free from their cages.

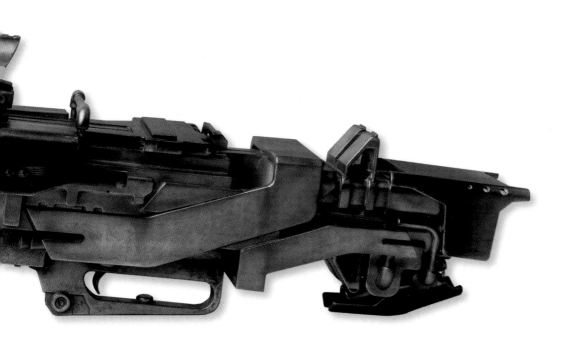

67

Gamora's Sword

Used by: Gamora

Years in use: Unknown to the present day

This formidable sword is wielded by Gamora, the adopted daughter of Thanos. She is brought into his Titan family when he and his Chitauri troops cleanse her home planet of half its population—all part of Thanos' heartless galactic rebalancing effort. Gamora is trained under Thanos' guidance to become an assassin, an expert in unarmed combat and deadly with a number of weapons, including her signature sword. This weapon is dangerous in multiple forms: it has a detachable knife that Gamora can

throw for long-range targeting, and it can also be split into two long blades for dual effectiveness at close range.

Gamora's exceptional fighting skills are made clear to both friends and foes, including foes that become friends on Xandar, when Groot, Rocket, Gamora, and Quill are on a wild chase in order to gain possession of either the Orb or a human bounty. During their first encounter, Groot's limbs are cut off by Gamora's mighty sword. Quill later finds himself at the pointed end of her sword as well, after a brief moment of attempted seduction. Gamora also turns her weapon on her own adoptive sister Nebula, not the first time the two have battled, as Thanos has a history of pitting the siblings against one another in order to hone their murderous skills.

Gamora's sword also proves effective on large-scale missions, such as when the Guardians of the Galaxy are assigned to protect the Anulax Battery supply of the Sovereign against the threat of the Abilisk. Gamora conquers this battery-eating monster with a deep cut to its throat-like region after Drax attempts to do the same from inside the creature. Gamora even has a chance to use her sword to attack Thanos in an alternate timeline, which ends, unfortunately, with her capture and the sword being taken into Quill's care thereafter.

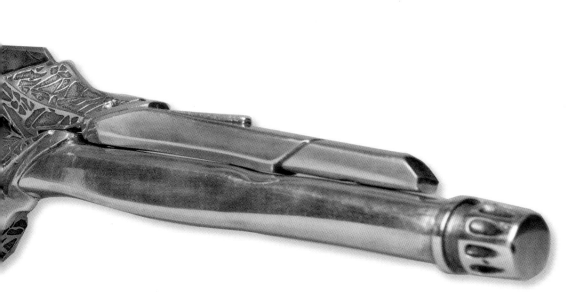

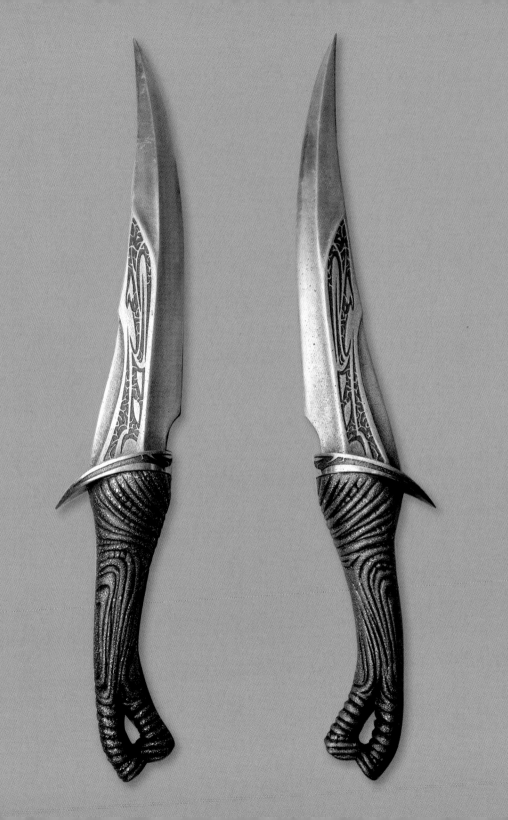

68

Drax's knives

Used by: Drax the Destroyer

Years in use: Unknown to the present day

This matched set of weapons is crafted from an unknown metal alloy, designed with clip point blades for stabbing, and finished with markings that echo the designs emblazoned on Drax's skin. For all the damage that Drax might threaten with his knives and his formidable strength, his aggression is balanced by a heart of gold that he exhibits when speaking of his love for his family and for the innocent creatures that he helps to free from the realm of the High Evolutionary as one of the Guardians of the Galaxy.

When not in use, the knives are housed in holsters on each of Drax's boots, ready to be drawn at a moment's notice. Drax has the confidence and capability to fight in hand-to-hand combat or utilize a blaster or sword-type weapon, but he is especially skilled with his knives. He has employed them to great effect in violent encounters around the galaxy. These include in battle aboard Ronan's battleship the *Dark Aster* to prevent the destruction of Xandar and against the Avengers—before he realizes they are also trying to defeat his ultimate enemy, Thanos. (Years before, Thanos had destroyed Drax's homeland, killing his wife and daughter in the process.)

Drax once again gets to channel his anger and revenge toward Thanos during the Avengers' Time Heist in 2023, serving as part of the team that finally undoes the destruction that Thanos has wrought on half of all the universe's life forms with his Snap.

69

Universal Weapon

Used by: Kree warrriors including Ronan and Dar-Benn
Years in Use: Unknown to the present day

This long-handled weapon is wielded by high-status Kree warriors such as Ronan the Accuser and Dar-Benn. Ronan uses his universal weapon to execute a Xandarian prisoner and Dar-Benn uses it to smash an ancient relic on the planet MP-148 to discover a Quantum Band. The weapon may be heaved or hurled at an opponent in hand-to-hand combat, as Dar-Benn exhibits in battle against Captain Marvel.

The universal weapon can also fire an energy blast, as Ronan demonstrates in Thanos' Sanctuary, inflicting a fatal blow on the Other when Thanos' servant questions Ronan's decision to dispatch Gamora to Xandar to obtain the Orb. Ronan recognizes that the energy of his weapon can be supplemented when merging it with another power source, using the Power Stone to boost its strength when in battle against the Nova Corps on Xandar. Later, at the moment of his seeming victory over the Xandarians, his glowing universal weapon is destroyed by a powerful gun blast, thanks to Star-Lord's cunning and Rocket's ingenuity.

Dar-Benn uses her weapon's energy to blast opponents and also to unleash ground-shaking blows, as Captain Marvel and Monica Rambeau experience when Dar-Benn encounters them on Aladna, and the Kree warrior also employs her weapon's energy to propel herself to higher ground. Dar-Benn eventually finds the combination of her universal

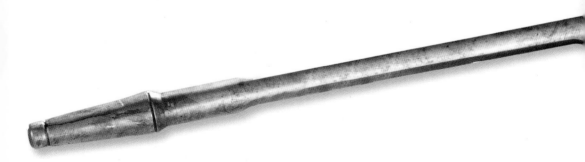

The universal weapon gains
extra power when merged
with another energy source.

weapon and the Quantum Band to be a powerful
tool for opening portals that tie into the Universal Neural
Teleportation Network, giving her a way to travel to other
planets on her quests for revenge or to steal life-sustaining
elements of air and water for her own dying homeworld, Hala.
When Dar-Benn obtains a pair of Quantum Bands, however,
the power-meld with her universal weapon proves
overwhelming, leading to her explosive demise.

70

Black Widow's Widow's Bite

Used by: Natasha Romanoff
Years in use: Unknown to 2018

Utilized by Natasha Romanoff, a.k.a. Black Widow, the Widow's Bite is a pair of wrist-mounted energy weapons integrated into her armored suit providing Black Widow with a versatile and potent tool. The Widow's Bite proves effective in most scenarios, complementing Black Widow's gamut of combat moves and skills.

In the late 20th century, Romanoff becomes an experienced warrior, trained in martial arts, numerous forms of weaponry, and espionage techniques through the Red Room program. She first uses her Widow's Bite when she shifts to working for S.H.I.E.L.D. She also employs an upgraded model developed by Stark Industries after she becomes an Avengers member in 2012.

The Widow's Bite gauntlets blend seamlessly into Black Widow's tactical gear. When activated, the gauntlets emit powerful electrical pulses that incapacitate opponents without causing permanent damage. The blue ray of energy dispensed by the Widow's Bite is effective at both short and long range and against large and small opponents.

During the conflict between the Avengers at Leipzig-Halle Airport, a downsized Ant-Man takes a hit at close range. In another clash, pirates who take over S.H.I.E.L.D.'s *Lemurian Star* are struck by pulses further away. One notable moment when Romanoff's Widow's Bite proves ineffective is against Crossbones, commander of a Hydra assault on the Institute for Infectious Diseases in Lagos.

Perhaps Black Widow's most intriguing use of her Widow's Bite occurs during the Avengers ambitious Time Heist, when she uses it against one of her dearest allies, Hawkeye. Romanoff then sacrifices herself so that Hawkeye can obtain the Soul Stone before Thanos does.

Whether black or gold
in color, all models of
the Widow's Bite pack
a powerful punch.

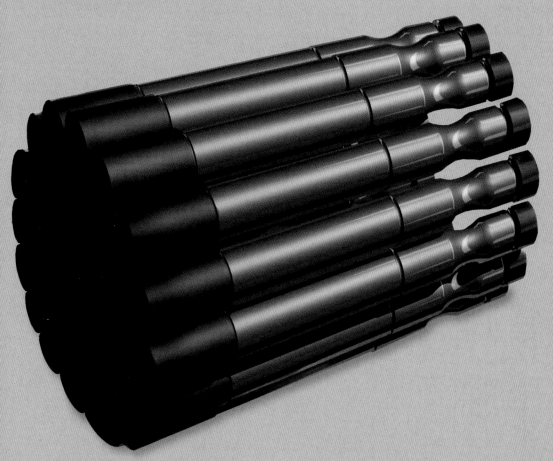

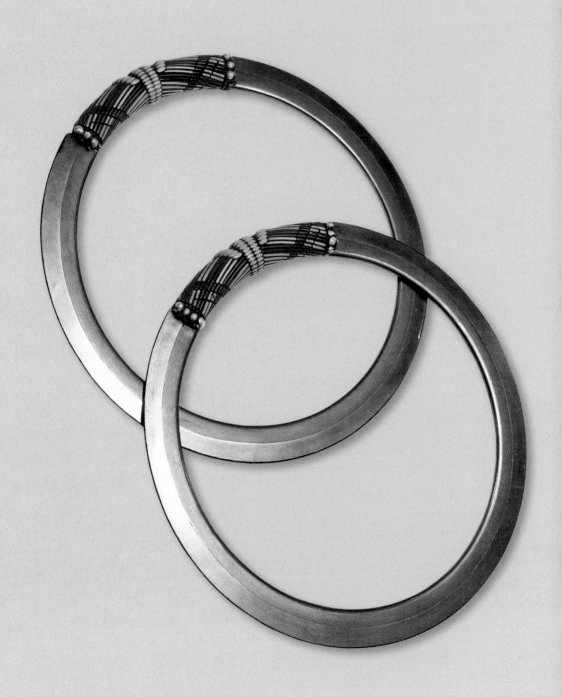

71

Circular
Vibranium Blades

Used by: Nakia

Years in use: Unknown to the present day

Nakia serves Wakanda as a secret intelligence officer, part of the War Dogs organization that works on assignments around the globe in order to protect their homeland from international threats. Her missions have taken her to Nigeria, South Korea, and to various remote locations. Wherever she is assigned, she utilizes her exceptional espionage, martial arts, and general combat skills.

Although her confrontations have seen her employ guns, her bare hands, and, occasionally, a high-heeled shoe, one of Nakia's prime weapons is a pair of circular blades with woven hand grips. These extremely sharp, flat vibranium rings can be used in either hand, one at a time or in tandem, to slice or bludgeon targets. A single ring can also serve as an effective weapon, as when Nakia gives one of her rings to Queen Ramonda when they are part of her entourage wandering into Jabari territory in the wake of N'Jadaka, a.k.a. Killmonger, temporarily taking power in Wakanda.

In yet another manifestation of the innovative work of the Wakandan Design Group, Shuri designs an upgraded version of the blades, the new model markedly evident by the glow of light the blades emit. These enhanced rings are first put into action when T'Challa returns and rallies his trusted allies to shut down Killmonger's plans to ship vibranium weapons around the world, a battle in which Nakia is able to hurl the circular blades at her chosen targets and have them rebound to her after they strike. She also makes good use of them in a ferocious battle with Talokanil warriors on the deck of the *Sea Leopard*.

72

N'Jadaka's Sword

Used by: Erik "Killmonger" Stevens a.k.a. N'Jadaka
Year in use: 2016

This sword is a signature weapon owned by Erik Stevens. Growing up in Oakland, California, Stevens suffers the devastating loss of his father, not understanding the full scope of betrayal his father wrought upon his homeland of Wakanda, which led to his demise.

Stevens chooses a career path through the black ops ghost unit of the U.S. military to gain assassination missions—practice for the retribution he intends to exact against the Wakandan hierarchy in his father's honor. Stevens earns the nickname "Killmonger," and brazenly wears his murderous achievements as markings on his body as an intimidating challenge when he draws his leaf-shaped sword to threaten his cousin T'Challa, the Black Panther, for the crown of Wakanda in 2016. With his leaf-shaped sword in one hand and a broken spear in the other, Stevens eventually sends T'Challa over the edge of a waterfall.

As N'Jadaka, King of Wakanda, he aims to take the country in a totally new direction by using vibranium weapons to dominate the globe, boasting, "The world's going to find out exactly who we really are." T'Challa surprisingly and spectacularly reappears as Black Panther, and literally causes N'Jadaka's forces to crash and burn. Undaunted, N'Jadaka draws his sword from the sling on his back and battle ensues on a grand scale between N'Jadaka's Border Tribe Warriors and the Dora Milaje, whose leader, Okoye, shouts at N'Jadaka, "Your heart is so full of hatred, you are not fit to be a king." Attired in his own Black Panther suit, N'Jadaka takes on four of the Dora Milaje singlehanded, seizing and mercilessly killing one of them with his favorite sword.

As N'Jadaka turns his wrath toward Shuri amidst the fray, T'Challa knocks him into a deep vibranium mine shaft. The two fight to the finish, each in Black Panther suits, with N'Jadaka going down in defeat as T'Challa delivers a final impaling blow.

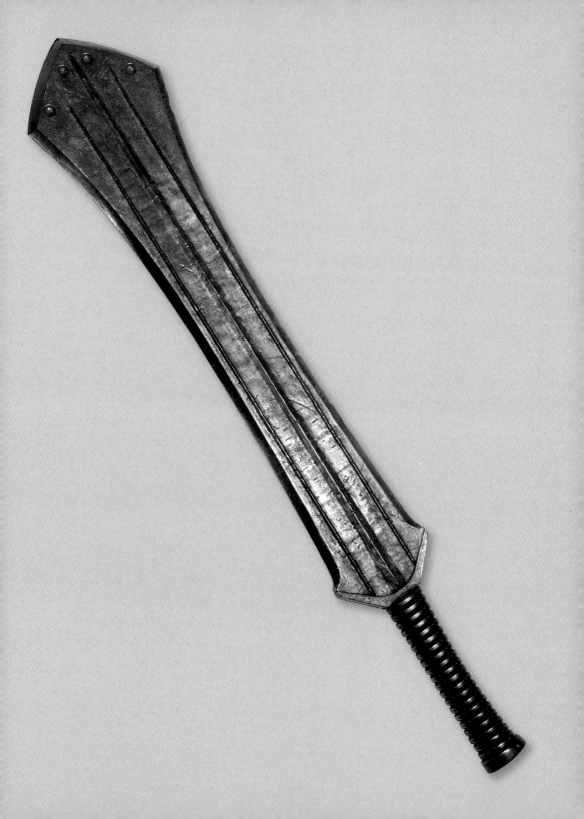

73

Vibranium Dagger

Used by: Aneka

Years in use: 2016 to the present day

The Dora Milaje are a formidable force of spear-carrying female warriors who serve to protect Wakanda's leadership and greater country. One of the well-trained and battle-hardened members of this Wakandan royal guard is Aneka, who numbers two vibranium daggers among her weapons.

While General Okoye would prefer that her warriors only wield the spear that their foremothers gave them for attack and defense, Aneka is also drawn to these newer weapons created by Shuri and the Wakandan Design Group. She first employs these glowing blue daggers when intruders break into a top-secret vibranium laboratory. With a smooth sweep, Aneka effortlessly slices through the invaders' metal artillery without encountering any notable resistance.

Aneka is later invited to fight alongside Okoye as a newly conceived warrior known as a Midnight Angel to confront the Talokanil, an underwater-living tribe from the Yucatan region that also values its precious vibranium resource and aims to keep it off the radar of international intruders at any cost. Aboard the grand Wakandan ship *Sea Leopard*, Aneka and her allies battle the Talokanil army in the Atlantic Ocean. Once again her vibranium daggers prove equal to the task at hand. In her Midnight Angel guise, Aneka uses her glowing daggers to remarkable effect, both at close quarters and also long distance, throwing them with incredible speed and accuracy. Furthermore, the daggers return to her, allowing Aneka to hit targets at some distance and to keep on using them—yet another of the innovative combat advantages provided by the work of the Wakandan Design Group.

74

Hela's Helmet

Used by: Hela, Goddess of Death
Years in use: Unknown to 2017

This impressive horned helmet adorned the head of Hela, the firstborn of Odin known for her path of conquest and ruthless treachery. Her destructive *modus operandi* suited Odin's early days on the throne, when Hela served as the Executioner of Asgard. But when Odin's attitude to his leadership role became less warlike, Hela refused to fall in line. Odin was forced to imprison her in order to cease her reign of terror. Hela remained in captivity until Odin's human body expired and his time on the earthly plane came to an end. In that moment of Odin's passing, Hela broke free from incarceration and came to surprise her younger siblings, Thor and Loki, who had no real understanding of her existence or evil tendencies. The brothers struggled to quell her wrath, which was powerful enough to take down the entire Asgardian army singlehanded.

Hela's hot-headed expression of authority was embodied in her helmet. As if her magically conjured arsenal of axes, swords, and other spiked weapons was not daunting enough, her headgear's wicked-looking antlers were the crowning glory of her threatening and imposing presence. Her power was seemingly insurmountable, drawing on the very essence of

Asgard for her energy; she was even able to crush Mjolnir with her bare hands. Thor sought battle reinforcement from the ex-pat Valkyrie, who had recast her life on Sakaar after Hela eliminated her fellow winged warriors long ago, but even Valkyrie's return was not enough to shut down Hela.

After Heimdall deftly evacuated innocent Asgardians from certain death, Thor and Valkyrie battled Hela and her resurrected undead army. When their efforts seemed futile, as a last resort Thor and Loki invoked Ragnarok, the prophesied fiery end of Asgard. The power source that Hela thrived upon was destroyed, presumably reducing her—in all her helmeted glory—to ashes with the rest of the realm.

75

Dragonfang Sword

Used by: Valkyrie

Years in use: The ancient past to the present day

Valkyrie is the last remaining warrior of a legendary powerful force of women in Asgard, a sisterhood that mightily serves their kingdom until the Goddess of Death, Hela, wipes out all but one of them in a rush of fury that is characteristic of her destructive nature and desire to conquer all.

Valkyrie distances herself from this torturous past and looming survivor's guilt by escaping to Sakaar, becoming scavenger Scrapper 142, a discontented servant of the planet's ruler, the Grandmaster. However, she does keep her trusty daggers and sword in her possession, some of which she pulls on Thor when he pleads with her to come back to protect her homeland from Hela. Once her loyalty to the people of Asgard is rekindled, Valkyrie relishes the idea of driving her sword through Hela, especially when Loki calls to her mind a flashback of the legion of Valkyrie battling Hela the first time—a fight that ended in a bitter defeat caused by Hela's casting of seemingly infinite swords.

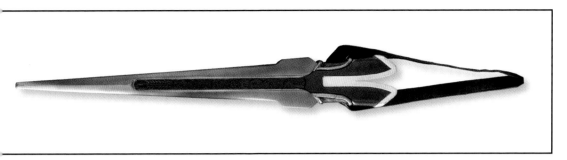

addition to Dragonfang,
alkyrie carries two daggers.

As Valkyrie, Thor, Loki, and Hulk steal a spacecraft to flee Sakaar in order to return to Asgard, Valkyrie wields her sword against the Sakaaran Guard ship that chases them. Arriving at Asgard, Valkyrie makes good use of her sword, piercing and beheading Hela's undead soldiers and thrusting Dragonfang through Hela herself, before the manifestation of Ragnarok finishes the job of sending Asgard—and more importantly, Hela's destructive dreams—up in flames.

During the Blip, Valkyrie helps to establish New Asgard on Earth. In 2023 she once again demonstrates her outstanding warrior prowess, unsheathing her mighty sword to fight alongside the Avengers and other allies in the epic battle against Thanos that succeeds in reversing the destruction of his Snap. In the aftermath of victory, Thor acknowledges her as King of New Asgard.

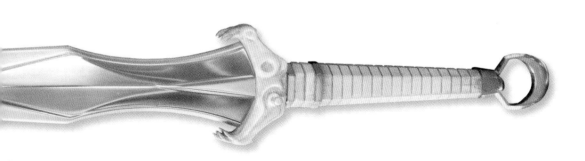

76

Executioner's Ax

Used by: Skurge

Year in use: 2017

This ax was wielded by Skurge in service to Hela, Goddess of Death's bid to rule Asgard. The weapon was magically manifested from her body in a fashion similar to the way she crafted her own arsenal of swords and blades. She demonstrated its effectiveness to Skurge by using it to smash a hole in the palace vault floor in order to access the crypt. This contained the corpses of warriors and the Fenris Wolf, all of whom Hela brought back to life with the Eternal Flame to serve as her undead army.

Skurge was a warrior who claimed to have fought alongside Thor at the battle of Vanaheim. After Heimdall was unfairly accused of negligence and forced to flee Asgard by Loki—shape-shifting to impersonate Odin—the unscrupulous Skurge gained the prestigious role of gatekeeper of the Bifrost.

Upon Hela's unexpected and deadly return to Asgard via the Bifrost, she took a liking to Skurge. He gained a first glimpse of her ruthlessness when she ordered the Asgardian army to obey her and join in her vision of conquest beyond the Nine Realms. When the soldiers—none of whom knew who she was—refused to recognize her right to rule, she killed them all. Hela later offered Skurge a prestigious job: to serve as her Executioner.

Skurge and his double-bladed ax induced terror and brought death on all who encountered them, until Skurge had a change of heart and conscience. In his final moments, Skurge courageously abandoned Hela's command and turned to battle her army in order to save his fellow Asgardians from certain death. His heroic efforts allowed the innocent citizens to gain entry to the transport ship *Statesman* and escape Ragnarok, which prophetically befell their homeland in the wake of Hela's rampage. Skurge and his ax were presumably both destroyed in the fiery destruction that followed.

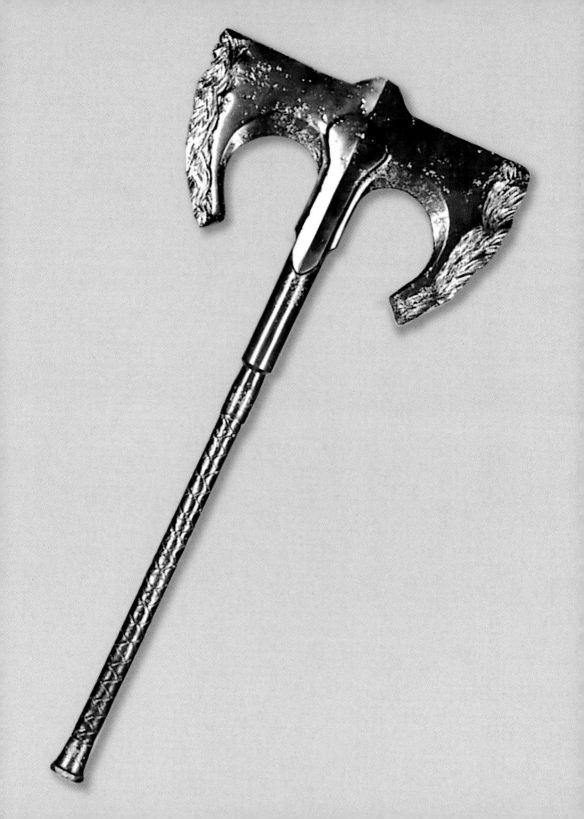

77

The Hulk's Arena Helmet

Used by: Hulk
Years in use: 2015 to 2017

This helmet is worn by the Hulk during his two-year stay on the planet Sakaar, which is surrounded by cosmic gateways and is the collection point for all lost and unloved things. Following his traumatic clash with Iron Man during a battle in Johannesburg in 2015, the Hulk seizes a Quinjet and crash-lands on Sakaar. The Hulk soon finds himself cast in a role that his superhuman physical prowess makes him particularly well suited for—as a mighty competitor in the Contest of Champions. This is a gladiatorial entertainment organized by Sakaar's autocratic ruler, the Grandmaster, to keep his people distracted from their downtrodden existence on a world that is little more than a gigantic junkyard.

The crowning glory of the Hulk's fighting attire is this metal helmet, which protected his skull, neck, and jaw from the impact of hand-to-hand combat. The headgear's crest gives it a gladiatorial appearance, reminiscent of combatants in the arenas of Ancient Rome.

The Hulk proudly sports this helmet when pitted against a contender for his title: Thor, propelled to Sakaar by the powers of Hela, Goddess of Death. If Thor can defeat the Grandmaster's champion, he will win his freedom. After a bruising contest, with the advantage swinging this way and that, the result is inconclusive, much to the Grandmaster's chagrin.

After a heart-to-heart chat with Thor, the Hulk metamorphoses back into Bruce Banner. He leaves Sakaar and his pampered life as the Grandmaster's champion to help Thor and Valkyrie vanquish Hela, who has taken power in Asgard.

Superior Science

The extraordinary objects in this section stretch the limits of human brainpower, inviting the question, "How is that possible?" The Marvel Cinematic Universe answers that question with, "It's science!" in a number of mind-boggling ways, from the incredible ingenuity informing a hero's armored battle suit, to the humanity-hating artificial intelligence of Ultron, and machines that can bring forth life or spread death and destruction at the push of a button.

78

Super Soldier Serum Vial

Used by: Dr. Erskine, numerous scientists, future super soldiers
Years in use: The 1940s to the present day

German scientist Dr. Abraham Erskine develops his Super Soldier Serum during World War II. When injected, cellular changes result in excruciating pain. Vita-Ray radiation stimulates the serum's effects, which greatly enhance the recipient's physical and mental abilities. As Erskine explains, "It amplifies everything that is inside, so good becomes great, bad becomes worse." Erskine's work intrigues Hydra officer Johann Schmidt. He uses an early version of the serum, causing a dark personality shift and the disfigurement that earns him the name the Red Skull.

After Erskine escapes to the U.S., the Allies enable him to continue his work. In 1943, he joins the Strategic Scientific Reserve to develop the serum. The scientist eventually encounters young, physically weak, but yearning-to-enlist Steve Rogers. By mutual agreement, Rogers becomes the test subject for Project Rebirth. The Super Soldier Serum is applied on June 22, 1943, and Captain America is born. Erskine is assassinated by Hydra soon after, and the secrets of his serum seemingly die with him.

In the ensuing decades, however, various scientists and organizations seek to replicate Erskine's formula. The Super Soldier Program is revived in the late 1940s, but with terrible outcomes for the African American soldiers experimented on against their will. The one exception is Isaiah Bradley, who nevertheless carries the mental scars for the rest of his life.

Hydra assassin the Winter Soldier later acquires five samples of the serum, increasing his deadly potential. The U.S. Army continues to meddle with the serum, in 2010 injecting the unfortunate Emil Blonsky, who receives a transfusion of the Hulk's blood and mutates into the Abomination. In 2024, the serum is stolen by the Flag Smashers and Sam Wilson, Bucky Barnes, and Baron Zemo ally to destroy the serum for good. A single vial survives, and is taken by John Walker—Captain America at that time. Unfortunately, the serum emphasizes Walker's violent tendencies, turning him into a killer.

79

The Tesseract

Used by: Odin, Johann Schmidt, Howard Stark, Mar-Vell, Erik Selvig,
S.H.I.E.L.D., Loki, Thanos
Years in use: The ancient past to 2018

The enigmatic cube structure called the Tesseract has been a coveted power source for eons, encompassing even the focus of S.H.I.E.L.D as part of Project Pegasus. The Tesseract's origin and the ancient civilizations to which it may have belonged precede all record keeping up until its stay in an historic church in Tønsberg, Norway, where the Asgardians placed it, hidden for centuries within a wooden carving that portrays Yggdrasil, the "Tree of the World." A fake Tesseract was placed in the coffin of a dead Viking warrior as a means of protecting the true resource.

In 1942, Hydra forces invade Norway and Johann Schmidt discovers the Tesseract then brings it into the Hydra lab for research under the watch of Dr. Arnim Zola. Hydra realizes it is an extremely powerful energy source, and applies it to their weapons technology, giving their forces an otherworldly advantage during World War II. Once Captain America infiltrates the Hydra facility and comes to realize that its plans to divebomb a plane powered with Tesseract-enhanced explosives into the United States, he takes matters into his own hands and manages to crash-land the plane into the depths of a polar ice cap instead. Search parties do not locate the remains of the plane and Captain America for 70 years, but Stark technology does track the energy emission from this incident and retrieves the Tesseract, bringing it into the possession of S.H.I.E.L.D.

Various scientists from diverse backgrounds work with the Tesseract under the auspices of S.H.I.E.L.D. including Wendy Lawson, known as Mar-Vell in her Kree culture, in the 1980s. Her work as part of Project Pegasus focuses on the development of a light-speed engine. This project also greatly affects U.S. Air Force Pilot Carol Danvers. She is brought in to test fly the Pegasus Asis aircraft in 1989 and genetically altered when the plane explodes, absorbing its unexpectedly released Tesseract energy. In 1995, Danvers makes the acquaintance of S.H.I.E.L.D. Agent Nick Fury, and the two uncover both Danvers' complex history of having become a

Kree hybrid since her air force pilot duty and the location of the Tesseract, on Lawson's laboratory in space. With the help of Lawson's longtime companion Goose, the Tesseract is collected and finds its way back to the S.H.I.E.L.D. facility on Earth after being swallowed by the feline-looking Flerken.

Later in 1995, Tesseract research continues at S.H.I.E.L.D. under the authority of Dr. Erik Selvig. In 2012, the Tesseract's surges attract the intergalactic attention of Thanos who sends Loki on a mission to acquire the powerful energy source. A portal opens from space, giving Loki and an accompanying Chitauri force access to Earth while giving the Avengers Initiative its first large-scale battle.

After Loki's attempt to collect the Tesseract for Thanos fails during this aggressive maneuver in New York, Thor brings the Tesseract to Asgard for safekeeping in the royal vault, and it remains there until Ragnarok is brought about in 2017, during which Loki secretly saves the Tesseract from the utter destruction visited upon Asgard.

The fake Tesseract —clasped in a dead Viking warrior's hands in a church in Tønsberg, Norway.

In 2018, Thanos picks up the trail of the Tesseract again, finally gaining possession of it after confronting Thor, Loki, and the Hulk on the captured *Statesman* airship that was meant to rescue Asgardians from harm during their homeland's destruction. It is in this moment of transfer that the true power of the Tesseract is surprisingly revealed: the cube has been the container for the Space Stone all along, one of the coveted Infinity Stones that Thanos aims to collect to bring about the Snap and rebalance the universe, according to his inhumane standards.

The Tesseract being monitored in a S.H.I.E.L.D. lab.

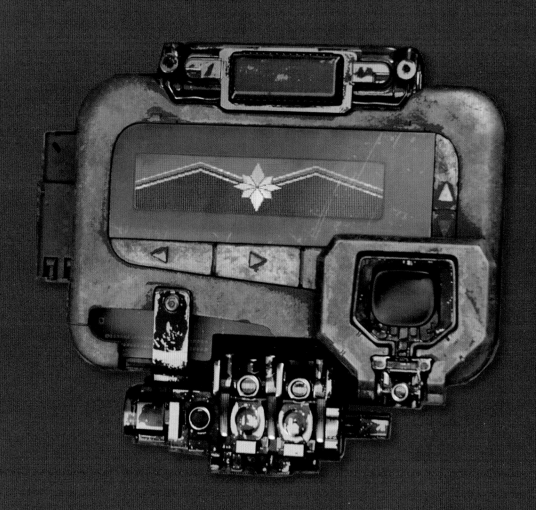

80

Captain Marvel's Pager

Used by: Captain Marvel, Nick Fury, the Avengers
Years in use: The 1990s to 2018

This unique piece of communications equipment is crafted by Captain Marvel and given to her newfound friend, S.H.I.E.L.D. Agent Nick Fury in 1995 before she departs Earth on a mission to find the Skrulls a new home. Not only does she convey great knowledge about civilizations beyond Earth to Fury in their short time together, but Captain Marvel also offers her continued support for the protection of the planet. She tells Fury that he can use the pager to contact her if dire threats arise.

Decades pass before Fury is compelled to use it. That moment comes during the onset of the Snap caused by Thanos and his Infinity Gauntlet in the spring of 2018. Fury is traveling with his colleague Maria Hill and witnesses her sudden disappearance—a chilling example of what half of Earth's inhabitants will endure in this catastrophic occurrence. He reaches out via the pager to his intergalactic ally—just before he himself falls victim to the Snap's vanishing effect.

When the Avengers that remain in existence after the Snap investigate Fury's disappearance, they discover this object and are puzzled by what it is and does. After continued efforts to keep the pager charged and communicating, Bruce Banner, Steve Rogers, Natasha Romanoff, and James Rhodes finally find the answer when the pager ceases to function and Captain Marvel suddenly appears and asks, "Where's Fury?" An important collaboration is thus formed: an alliance between Captain Marvel and the Avengers to protect Earth and other vulnerable inhabitants of the universe.

Once Fury is restored following the Blip, his workplace shifts to an interspace station defense system known as the Strategic Aerospace Biophysics and Exolinguistic Response (S.A.B.E.R.). There he uses other, even more advanced technology, to stay in contact with Captain Marvel.

81

Tony Stark's Workshop Robots

Used by: Tony Stark, Happy Hogan

Years in use: 1986 to the present day

These two similar hydraulic-armed robots were created by the genius of Tony Stark in the mid 1980s. In this era, Stark was described as a "wunderkind," being only 16 years of age and an innovative student.

Stark's technological skills enabled him to create two robots, known as Dum-E and Dum-U. These helpful companions served as his partners during his creation of his Iron Man Mark II armor—a significant upgrade on his original armor.

Even more importantly, on one occasion Dum-E helps to save Stark's life. When Stark's business partner Obadiah Stane rips the Arc Reactor from Stark's chest in order to power his own Iron Monger armor, Dum-E hands the virtually helpless Stark an earlier model of Arc Reactor to implant into his body and keep his heart beating.

Dum-U is not the neatest chef when a blender is involved, but it's great at filming the Iron Man development process, capturing various successes and failures along the way up through Mark 52, vital archiving to Stark's creative efforts. Dum-U also shows it can be of more refined service, successfully delivering a tray of champagne in a moment of celebration for Pepper Potts' appointment to CEO of Stark Industries.

After suffering injury when Stark Mansion is blown apart during an unsuccessful assassination attempt in 2013, the robots are rebuilt by Stark. Although the whereabouts and fate of Dum-U are unknown, Dum-E outlasts Stark's time on Earth, later coming into Happy Hogan's possession and moving to his condominium.

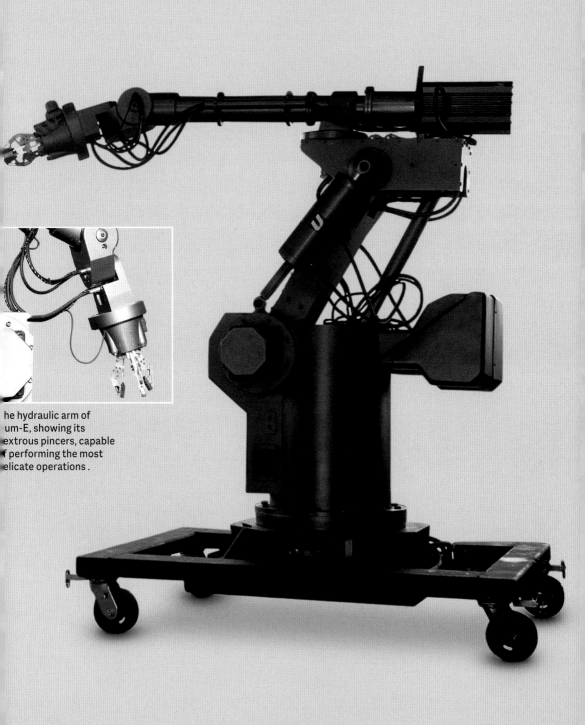

The hydraulic arm of um-E, showing its extrous pincers, capable f performing the most elicate operations .

82

Iron Man Armor

Used by: Tony Stark
Years in use: 2008 to 2023

Tony Stark has the mind and the means to build nearly anything he desires. One of his proudest accomplishments is his suite of Iron Man armors, improved over and over in model upgrades over the course of 15 years. The Iron Man armors are metal-hewn flying warrior suits, originating from a concept Stark developed while held captive in 2008 in Afghanistan by The Ten Rings organization.

Prior to his capture, Stark was wounded in a bomb explosion caused by The Ten Rings. He is fortunate to be incarcerated alongside the scientist Dr. Ho Yinsen, who deftly performs an operation that involves the installation of an electromagnet in Stark's chest that prevents pieces of embedded shrapnel from reaching his heart and killing him. Their Ten Rings captors then instruct them to build a Jericho missile, but instead Stark secretly crafts a miniature Arc Reactor and an escape pod out of the materials provided, and these components become the initial build of an Iron Man suit. The rig is a shell of metal fitted to encase Stark's body that effectively transforms him into a walking tank, deflecting bullets and blows and the heat of fire. The battle suit blasts flaming energy from both arms, launches small missiles from the left arm, and propels itself for a short flight out of The Ten Rings' compound and to freedom.

After Stark is recovered by U.S. forces in the deserts of Afghanistan, he is inspired to publicly share the news that he plans to shift Stark Industries' production away from weapons production and focus on other work. He informs his business partner, Obadiah Stane, that he means to place more emphasis on Arc Reactor technology.

Meanwhile, Stark privately continues to develop his Iron Man concept, working offline from Stark Industries on his Mark II armor, a new build of the rig using the full resources of his lab and the power of the Arc Reactor technology. Working with the support of his robots Dum-U and Dum-E as well as his A.I. partner JARVIS, Stark builds and tests multiple aspects of the suit, including its thrust capacity, visual interface, and overall construction. On a clear night, Stark takes this sleek silver version for its

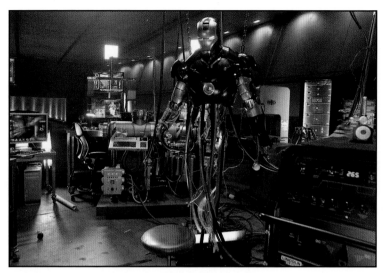

Iron Man's armor benefits from Stark's focus on constant innovation. Here the Mark III takes shape in his lab.

first flight, circling Santa Monica pier and testing the limits of its speed and altitude range.

Stark's Mark III armor is the model that first exhibits the iconic "hot rod red" on top of a golden base, and it is this version that Stark takes into battle after watching news coverage of the plight of refugees affected by The Ten Rings's activities. He is particularly moved by the pleas of a child displaced from his mother and father, which echo his own experience of being orphaned after the assassination of his parents. The Mark III can not only circumnavigate the globe, it can punch through walls, fire multiple bullets at multiple targets simultaneously, take a hit from high-powered weaponry, launch a tank-exploding missile from its right arm, blast enough power from its palm thrusters to detonate a trio of Jericho missiles, and outmaneuver startled American fliers with missile lock capabilities.

Later in 2008, Stark is approached by Nick Fury, Director of S.H.I.E.L.D., who proposes that Iron Man become part of the Avengers Initiative. From that point forward, Stark applies his skills and energy in collaboration with a fleet of fellow protectors of the world. He continues to develop his Iron Man technology and that of his fellow Avengers until 2023. Wearing his Mark 85 armor—featuring nanotechnology and countless upgrades from the Mark I version—Stark successfully undoes the damage Thanos has wrought upon Earth five years prior with the Snap of his Infinity Gauntlet. Sadly, this achievement costs Stark his life.

A few of the models that Stark built during
a 15-year focus on Iron Man missions.

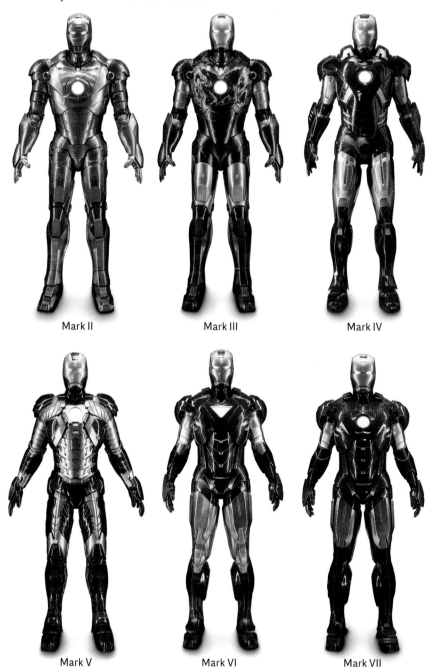

Mark II   Mark III   Mark IV

Mark V   Mark VI   Mark VII

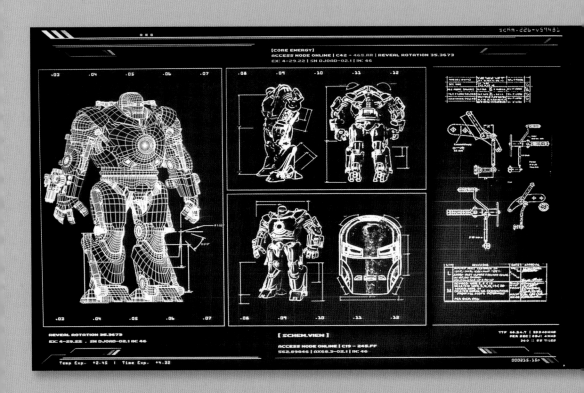

83

"Iron Monger" Armor Blueprint

Used by: Obadiah Stane
Year in use: 2008

This blueprint exists courtesy of Obadiah Stane, who serves as Howard Stark's business partner in Stark Industries, and then rises to interim CEO after Howard's death in 1991. It's a position of power he enjoys until Howard's son Tony Stark enters the picture, and then Stane resents the younger Stark's presence so much that he plans an assassination attempt that includes a kidnapping by The Ten Rings in Afghanistan. When Tony Stark miraculously escapes from his captors by building an early version of Iron Man armor from scrap metal, Stane is further infuriated. He acquires the remnants of Stark's Iron Man armor and pressures a team of his own scientists and engineers to build a bigger, stronger version, known as the "Iron Monger." However, Stane's team fails to eradicate some of the Iron Man armor's original shortcomings.

In order to power up his Iron Monger suit, Stane steals the miniature Arc Reactor from Stark's chest. When this highly invasive act does not finish off Stark, Stane dons his Iron Monger armor to take on Iron Man directly. He blazes away at close range with the machine gun housed in his suit's right arm, and uses the laser target and missile launcher in the left shoulder of the suit to attempt to catch and destroy the smaller, more nimble Iron Man.

After Stane uses the rocket boosters housed in the Iron Monger's boots to chase Stark to high altitudes, the suit experiences technical difficulties with freezing temperatures—something Stark's original suit had not had to contend with. However, that is not enough to halt Stane's attack: Stark orders Pepper Potts to fire up Stark Industries' full-scale Stark Industries Arc Reactor. The Iron Monger Armor is blown to pieces and Stane with it.

84

Gamma-Radiation Detector

Used by: Dr. Bruce Banner
Years in use: The early 2000s to the present day

Dr. Bruce Banner is a brilliant scientist with an impressive seven doctorates to his name, and his unique combination of knowledge in biochemistry, computer science, engineering, mathematics, nuclear physics, radiophysics, and robotics makes him a valuable resource for research efforts undertaken by the U.S. Army. When he is recruited, he is told his work will help protect soldiers from the effects of nuclear radiation. However, Banner finds himself involved in a secret effort to resurrect the Super Soldier Program—work that had been paused decades prior. Banner's approach involves electromagnetic radiation known as gamma radiation, and thus machinery such as this gamma-radiation detector becomes a vital part of his work. Unfortunately, when Banner proceeds to test the gamma radiation dosage on himself, his experiments lead to him absorbing a massive dose of gamma rays. At moments of high-tension, these gamma rays trigger a dramatic physical and psychological transformation, turning Banner into a giant with a limitless propensity for violence who becomes known as the Hulk.

While Banner grapples with managing his Hulk outbursts over the years, he is still revered as a scientist and in 2012 is recruited by S.H.I.E.L.D. to assist in efforts to locate the Tesseract, owing to its gamma-radiation emissions. From that point forward, Banner is brought into the Avengers Initiative and adds both his scientific acumen and his strength to their varied missions.

One of Banner's bravest acts is to offer to handle the Infinity Stones during the Avengers' Time Heist in 2023, knowing that he is best suited to the task owing to his tolerance for gamma radiation and strength in Hulk form. Banner's effort in the lab preparing the Avengers' version of a gauntlet, in combination with Iron Man's ultimate version of a Snap, reverses the damage wrought by Thanos five years prior.

85

Hawkeye's Trick Arrows

Used by: Clint Barton

Years in use: Unknown to the present day

Whether as a S.H.I.E.L.D. agent, as Hawkeye in the Avengers, or as the vigilante Ronin during the Blip, Clint Barton frequently supplements his peerless archery skills with a quiver containing an extraordinary variety of specialized arrows. Depending on the mission, Barton may load up with a single or a double-barreled quiver. For example, when, in 2010, he is assigned by S.H.I.E.L.D. a bird's-eye-view watch of the Mjolnir crash site, he has only a single quiver slung across his back as his only potential target is Thor, who breaks into the classified S.H.I.E.L.D. zone to try to reclaim his mighty hammer. Although Barton is as watchful as a hawk from high above, his special skills are not put into play, on the orders of supervising S.H.I.E.L.D. agent Phil Coulson.

For a much larger-scale event, however, such as when Loki and a fleet of Chitauri attack New York City in an attempt to claim the Tesseract from the scientists of S.H.I.E.L.D. in 2012, Hawkeye successfully targets numerous alien intruders from his rooftop perch, employing a double-quiver of trick arrows. As well as standard projectiles that pick off single Chitauri opponents, Hawkeye fires explosive arrows at airships (including Loki's), and launches one with a grapple point that allows him to leap from the edge of a building, swing by the attached cable, and crash through a window to an interior floor below.

During an earlier part of this great battle, Barton is under the mind control of Loki and uses a navigationally enhanced, remote-controlled detonator arrow to take out an engine of the S.H.I.E.L.D. Helicarrier. He follows that with explosive arrows to blast crew out of the way in the Helicarrier's control room, and finally a data-extraction arrow to shut down some of its computer systems. Happily, Barton rights these wrongs once his mind is back in the right place.

When the Avengers seek to take out a Hydra research base in Sokovia in 2015, Hawkeye again utilizes his full double-barreled quiver and

launches well-placed arrows while riding atop an SUV, destroying bunkers with explosive arrows. When battling Ultron, Hawkeye is seen shooting a fusillade of explosive arrows as well as triple and double arrows in the heat of conflict, effective even when holding a conversation with Wanda Maximoff at the same time.

When Barton and his protégé Kate Bishop—who has adopted Barton's old Ronin outfit—team up to battle the Tracksuit Mafia in New York City in 2024, their joint efforts involve arrows shot two at a time to pin an opponent to a wall, two arrows delivered simultaneously by hand instead of by bow, stopping pursuers in their tracks by piercing their feet, and one carefully targeted from afar to untie

Hawkeye employs his double-barreled quiver on larger-scale missions.

Hawkeye's formidable Avengers arsenal.

Bishop's hands. Mid-car chase, with Hawkeye driving and Bishop on weapons duty, Bishop launches arrows that emit purple putty, explosions, a web of cables, and a purple gas.

Once their vehicle is no longer moving, the duo work together as Bishop launches a conventional arrow that Barton then super-sizes by targeting it with a Pym-Particle-tipped arrow. The result is a single giant-size arrow that brings an oncoming truck to a shuddering halt.

In another showdown with the Tracksuit Mafia, Bishop launches a fire arrow, an arrow that spins and sends off spikes in all directions, and a navigationally enhanced lasso- and jet pack-capable arrow, while Barton reaches into his quiver to launch an ice-inducing arrow, a taser-band arrow, and a gas-emitting arrow, as well as an arrow that can split mid-flight to hit three targets simultaneously.

A small selection of the many trick arrows that Hawkeye has at his disposal in battle.

86

Dr. Erik Selvig's Phase Meter

Used by: Dr. Erik Selvig, Dr. Jane Foster, Darcy Lewis, Ian Boothby
Years in use: Unknown to the present day

Dr. Erik Selvig is a well-respected—if eccentric—scholar in theoretical astrophysics whose vast inventory of equipment includes a device called a Phase Meter. This machine measures cosmic energy, a vital part of the studies he and his mentee Dr. Jane Foster use in their work.

Dr. Selvig's discoveries about mythology and the cosmos align in 2010 when he and Foster encounter Thor and the Bifrost, which Thor uses to traverse the two realms of Earth and Asgard. When a portal such as the Bifrost opens, there is a notable shift in levels of energy in nearby space.

Dr. Selvig's Phase Meter proves especially useful in 2013, when a massive alignment of portals emerges in an area of Southeast London. Outside of the Old Royal Naval College in Greenwich, Dr. Foster, Darcy Lewis, and Ian Boothby set up the Phase Meter. Its intriguing readings lead them to an abandoned warehouse, where the appearance of portals becomes obvious. The team later comes to realize that what is taking place is the Convergence, an event that only occurs once in every 5,000 years, which Dr. Selvig had previously theorized.

This alignment of portals to all Nine Realms in the universe is more than an earthly scientific anomaly—it is also an opportunity for the King of the Dark Elves, Malekith, to attempt to fulfill his yearning for eternal darkness to encompass all existence. Foster personally encounters the power of the Aether, the weapon that the Dark Elves need in order to bring Malekith's plan to fruition. Between Foster's absorption of the Aether's power and Thor's physical battle with Malekith—which brings another of Dr. Selvig's devices, the gravimetric spikes, into play—the Dark Elves' expansion of darkness fails.

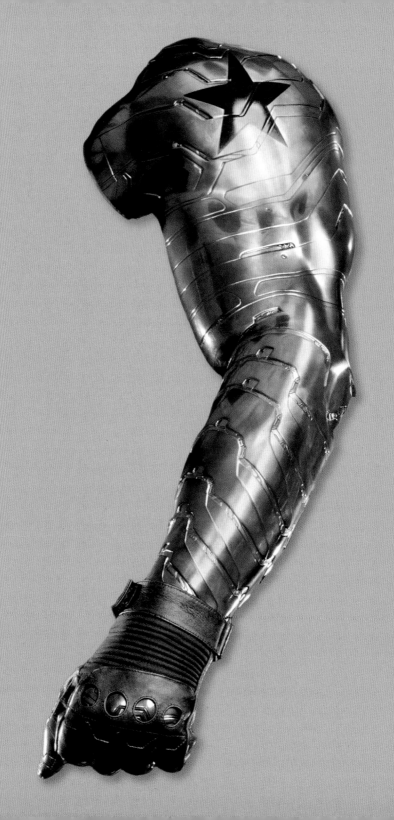

87

Winter Soldier's Bionic Arm

Used by: James Buchanan "Bucky" Barnes
Years in use: The late 1940s to the present day

This bionic arm is an integral part of the weaponry of the Winter Soldier, the assassin developed by Hydra in the Soviet Union during the 1940s. The Winter Soldier is created using James Buchanan "Bucky" Barnes as its unwilling human basis. Having enlisted in the Army during World War II, Barnes is captured during a mission to track down Hydra scientist Dr. Arnim Zola. In a cruel reversal of fortune, Zola masterminds the conversion of Barnes into a killing machine using a combination of Super Soldier Serum, brainwashing, and a powerful bionic arm. This is specially created by Hydra to replace Barnes' left arm, amputated following a fall from a train during his failed mission.

The Winter Soldier's bionic arm becomes a key component of his *modus operandi*. He uses it in numerous clashes, including ripping open a S.H.I.E.L.D. armored vehicle, and tearing apart Falcon's wingsuit. This model of bionic arm is finally destroyed in battle with Iron Man in 2016.

Barnes' surprise reunion with childhood friend and former fellow Howling Commando Steve Rogers leads to his eventual awakening from Hydra's brainwashing, and, in 2018, a vibranium replacement is crafted by innovative Wakandan engineer Shuri. Barnes' focus switches to making amends for past wrongs and serving alongside the Avengers.

This new arm becomes a point of fascination for Rocket after they fight side-by-side in Wakanda attempting to keep Thanos from achieving his Infinity Gauntlet goal. Years later, Rocket's wish to possess the arm comes true when Nebula gifts him it for Christmas 2025, leaving others to wonder what sort of handshake deal Nebula must have worked out with the Winter Soldier to make that happen.

88

Star-Lord's Helmet

Used by: Peter Quill, Gamora
Years in use: Unknown to 2026

Half-human, half-Celestial, Peter Quill has spent most of his life in space, having been abducted from planet Earth as a boy by Ravagers. Quill learns to adapt to intergalactic living, facilitated by vital equipment such as the helmet he sometimes wears as part of his self-created hero persona, Star-Lord. His helmet is activated by touching an earpiece he wears on his right side. Following a surface mapping of blue energy, the metal-looking helmet wraps around Quill's head. It helps Quill breathe in deep space and on foreign planet atmospheres while also offering physical protection. The helmet also contains audio communications technology and a multitude of visual analytics and enhanced imaging that link to gadgets Quill uses. Statistics and readouts appear on its interior view. With its red, glowing eyes the helmet also gives Star-Lord a more mysterious and intimidating appearance—an impression Quill is keen to project when establishing his reputation as a "famous outlaw," and, later, as a Guardian of the Galaxy.

Star-Lord has proved his heroic credentials through a number of self-sacrificing acts. One of the most notable is when he leaves the safety of his flight pod and gives his helmet to help Gamora breathe when she is drifting in deep space. Fortunately, he and Gamora are hauled aboard the Ravagers' ship before they both expire.

Although this version of his helmet is cracked and broken after Quill battles his Celestial father, Ego, Star-Lord has another one ready when he joins the Avengers to battle Thanos in 2018. This helmet disintegrates along with him during the Blip, reappears with him after the Avengers' Time Heist succeeds in 2023, and is finally shelved in 2026. It is not needed when Quill returns to Earth to spend time with the last surviving member of his human family, his grandfather Jason.

89

Ultron's Destroyed Body

Used by: Ultron
Year in use: 2015

Ultron is an artificial intelligence that takes an extremely wrong turn from the path intended by its human creators, Tony Stark and Bruce Banner. Instead of serving as a global peacekeeping system meant to protect Earth from aggressive intergalactic intruders, Ultron morphs into a megalomaniacal machine seeking to exterminate the Avengers and all humankind along with them.

The intelligence initially installs himself into a bundle of remnant robotic parts from the Stark Legion drones and adds other Stark robotic creations to his forces, much to the Avengers' surprise. After a ferocious battle at the Avengers Tower, Ultron's body is smashed to pieces by Thor's hammer, which unfortunately only eliminates Ultron in a single physical manifestation as his virtual intelligence rampages through the internet.

Ultron next occupies a body crafted from Chitauri relics collected at a Hydra research base in Sokovia, upping his weaponry and mobility capabilities. The A.I. allies with Wanda and Pietro Maximoff to craft more robotic Sentinels to strengthen his forces and further divide the attention of the Avengers, while he also creates a doomsday trigger device that will cause a devastating meteoric impact to the world.

Ultron also aspires to have the brilliant Dr. Helen Cho build the ultimate body at her lab in Seoul to serve as his next level presence, a humanoid honed out of vibranium and finished off with the Mind Stone set in its head. When the Avengers thwart this attempted embodiment, Ultron moves forward with his doomsday plan and is nearly successful in its implementation until Ultron's former ally, Wanda Maximoff, rips his mechanical heart from his latest robotic body. Simultaneously, Iron Man and Thor explode the launched landmass-turned-meteor before it falls back to Earth, thus ending the legacy of Ultron as well.

Ultron confronts the Avengers for the first time and accuses them of being "all killers."

The Regeneration Cradle creates the synthezoid Vision.

90

Regeneration Cradle

Used by: Dr. Helen Cho, for work on Clint Barton, Ultron, and Vision
Years in use: Unknown to 2015

This piece of innovative medical technology is named for its ability to regenerate tissue to support the healing processes of the human body. The Regeneration Cradle is the creation of Dr. Helen Cho of the U-GIN Genetics Infinite Research and Development facility in Seoul, South Korea. A Stark Labs-based version of its technology set up by Dr. Cho proves successful after Clint Barton (alias Hawkeye) is severely injured in combat against Hydra forces in Sokovia in April 2015.

The work of Dr. Cho catches the attention of Ultron, the artificial intelligence crafted in Stark Labs as a peace-keeping effort by scientist Bruce Banner and inventor Tony Stark. Ultron, whose focus becomes corrupted and instead aims to annihilate humankind, inhabits a Stark sentry unit and escapes from Stark Labs.

Ultron later approaches Dr. Cho in her Seoul lab and mind-controls her to use her original Regeneration Cradle to generate a new full body for himself, built on a virtually indestructible vibranium base. This process is interrupted when the Avengers arrive and shut down Ultron's attempt to upload his intelligence into the new body. Ultron escapes to continue his path of destruction elsewhere using his current body and fellow sentries, while the Regeneration Cradle is transported to the Avengers Tower. The Avengers have a robust discussion as to how to eliminate the growing threat of Ultron. Given a power boost by Thor, the Regeneration Cradle is used to complete the creation of a synthezoid using Stark's JARVIS A.I. intelligence as its protocol center. The Regeneration Cradle explodes after this high-stakes task is complete, with Vision coming to synthesized life as its final piece of production.

91
Doomsday Trigger

Used by: Ultron
Years in use: 2015

This structure is a weapon of mass destruction designed by the artificial intelligence Ultron to be the means to bring humanity to an end. Ultron is the technological wonder created by Tony Stark to protect Earth from violent intergalactic invasions. Instead of serving as the universal peacekeeping entity that Stark had conceived, Ultron sees humanity as dangerous and fallible, and thus a major threat to peace. With remorseless logic, Ultron decides to remake the world and destroy humankind.

Ultron implants his intelligence in various robotic bodies to increase his physical presence and power, starting with one of Stark's Iron Legion drones and then a Chitauri-based droid in Sokovia. The A.I. later attempts to inhabit an even more impressive vibranium body created by Dr. Helen Cho. Fortunately this plan is thwarted by the Avengers and the vibranium body becomes the Avengers ally Vision.

Utilizing smuggled vibranium, Ultron assembles his doomsday detonation device beneath a deserted church in Sokovia's capital. When triggered, the doomsday mechanism is meant to lift the entire city from the ground, transport it to great heights, then smash it back to Earth, creating an asteroid-like wave of destruction.

The Avengers battle waves of former Hydra robots that Ultron has commandeered. Wanda Maximoff, seeking revenge on Ultron for killing her brother Pietro, rips out Ultron's mechanical heart. Meanwhile, Iron Man and Thor team up to strike at the core of the doomsday trigger with their combined power. They ultimately reduce the risen-city-turned-meteor into shattered pieces that cause far less damage on impact with the planet, thus saving humanity from Ultron's apocalyptic master plan.

92

The Ant-Man Suit

Used by: Hank Pym, Scott Lang
Years in use: The 1970s to the present day

As his code name suggests, Ant-Man embodies the power, strength and—sometimes—the size of ants. He does this by utilizing the intense effects of quantum energy that Dr. Hank Pym researched for decades.

In the 1970s, during his tenure with S.H.I.E.L.D., Pym focuses his work in the field of quantum energy. He calls his greatest discovery Pym Particles, a formula that involves subatomic components that can alter the distance between atoms, resulting in altered sizes for both living and inanimate objects. Pym's fellow innovator Howard Stark calls his particle work "the most revolutionary science ever developed." Historic film shows its devastating potential in warfare when a small, besuited, immensely strong creature appears to take down military detachments.

In 1987, Pym is called upon to assist in a mission to stop a Soviet missile aimed at the U.S. He and his wife Janet Van Dyne don special suits and use Pym Particles to shrink to ant size while maintaining their original strength and resilience.

The mission eventually owes its success to Janet, who reduces herself to an even smaller, subatomic level, entering the Quantum Realm in order to infiltrate and disarm the missile. Unfortunately, this courageous act of self-sacrifice prevents her from returning to normal reality from the Quantum Realm after saving the day and maintaining peace between the U.S. and Soviet Union. Pym blames himself for the loss of his beloved wife, as does his daughter, Hope Van Dyne.

Two years later, Pym feels his research risks are being compromised by certain less principled directors of S.H.I.E.L.D. and removes his Pym Particle research and remaining suit from that agency, secretly continuing to develop its potential in his private laboratory.

In 2015, Pym realizes that his protégé-turned-corporate usurper Darren Cross is seeking to interest Hydra in Pym Particle technology, having created his own powerful Yellowjacket battle suit. Pym arranges for a younger, more nimble man to steal and unknowingly inherit his Ant-Man suit in order to counteract Cross, and setting the path for ex-con Scott Lang to become the

The original Ant-Man helmet designed by Hank Pym,
as seen in his 1970s laboratory at Camp Lehigh.

next Ant-Man. Under the guidance of Hank Pym's no-nonsense daughter Hope Van Dyne, Lang learns martial arts and, more importantly, how the suit is meant to work symbiotically with its wearer. He also learns how to deal with the great mental and physical toll of rapid reductions and increases in size and body weight.

Lang eventually masters how to time his size changes to his benefit and his adversaries' detriment. He also ventures into the Quantum Realm on occasion like Janet Van Dyne, but has more advanced Pym technology at his fingertips to help him return to normal size than she did in the 1980s.

Additional tech includes a belted-on container of Pym Particle discs for changing the size of any object Lang wishes and particle-releasing button functions built into his suit for sudden personal size shifts. A regulator device on the belt and a monitor on the left gauntlet help to manage and track particle levels within the suit, and a gauntlet monitor displays his vital signs.

Tapping into the ant realm, the helmet of the Ant-Man suit also includes a Pym-designed earpiece that translates the wearer's brainwaves into electro-magnetic waves. These stimulate the olfactory nerves of ants, enabling the wearer to give them commands. Lang may lack Pym's natural fascination and depth of study of the ant kingdom, but he trains assiduously, working out physically underground with his ant allies and practicing telepathic communication with them via the earpiece. His first achievement is commanding a small ant team to flip and spin a penny. Soon he is leading an army of ants, often zooming through the air mounted on a flying ant.

Lang wears various upgraded versions of the Ant-Man suit in a wide range of scenarios before and after becoming a member of the Avengers. He even attempts to continue some of Pym's scientific work when the Snap causes the scientist to temporarily disappear from existence.

Scott Lang comes across the Ant-Man suit and helmet when he breaks into Hank Pym's home. Little does he know the discovery will totally transform his life.

93

The Wasp Prototype Suit

Used by: Hank Pym, Hope Van Dyne
Years in use: Unknown to the present day

Dr. Hank Pym focuses his research on quantum energy for decades, working for S.H.I.E.L.D. in the 1970s where he develops Pym Particles, a formula that affects the distance between atoms and allows for size manipulation of both living and inanimate objects. He expands upon his work by crafting suits that can withstand such size manipulation and protect the human body in the process.

These suits are worn by both Pym and his wife, Janet Van Dyne, when they embark on a top-secret mission in 1987 to disarm a Soviet missile headed for the U.S. Unfortunately, Janet does not return from that mission, as she slips into the Quantum Realm when she is compelled to downsize to subatomic levels to infiltrate the missile's structure and disarm it. Following the tragedy of her disappearance, Pym stops work on The Wasp prototype suit for decades.

The Wasp suit appears to contain similar wings to the "flying ant" suit Janet wears on that dangerous missile mission with her husband. However, it also offers advanced features, including stinger-like blasters on the wrists that allow the wearer to fire stunning power blasts at a target—not unlike the effect that thrown Pym Particle discs have on impact.

After Ant-Man Scott Lang manages to emerge safe and sound from the
Quantum Realm, Pym wonders if the work he and his wife were doing on
The Wasp suit is meant to be completed for their daughter Hope to use
—after all, she has proved to be a talented trainer in bringing Lang up to
speed to follow in her father's path as Ant-Man. Pym and Hope agree that
she should have the opportunity to follow her mother's example as The
Wasp, with the ultimate goal of rescuing Janet from the Quantum Realm.

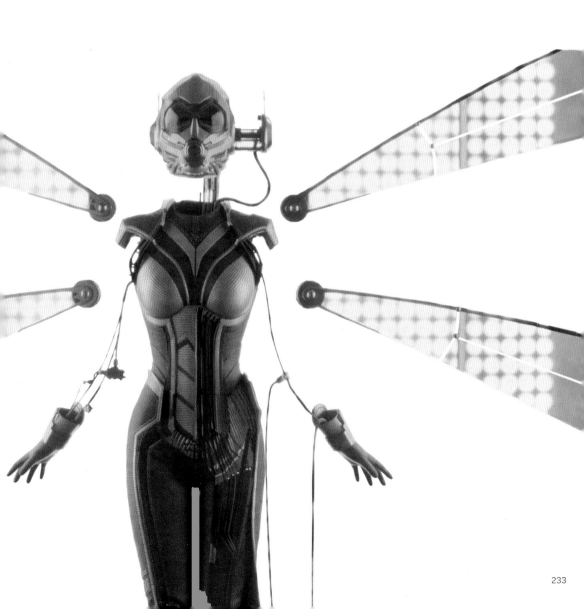

94

Pym's Shrunken Laboratory

Used by: Hank Pym, Hope Van Dyne, Scott Lang, Ava Starr, Bill Foster
Years in use: 2015 to the present day

Renowned scientist Dr. Hank Pym has worked in a lab as prestigious as the S.H.I.E.L.D. research facility, but moves to his own Pym Tech headquarters after he takes his quantum energy work out of the government realm and into his own development space. After the Sokovia Accords are put into effect, however, Pym is forced to take himself and his work into hiding as he is wanted for his creation of the Ant-Man persona, now considered criminal behavior under the international legislative agreement.

In an effort to remain effective yet undetected, Pym applies his size manipulation practices via the use of Pym Particles to his home, his fleet of vehicles, and also to his research laboratory in order to stay off the radar of the authorities seeking to put a stop to his work. While the lab may be small enough to be considered carry-on-appropriate travel-size luggage, it is far more valuable than that, according to those that desperately want to obtain it. They include Pym's former co-worker Dr. Bill Foster and his mentee, young S.H.I.E.L.D. agent Ava Starr, who suffers from molecular disequilibrium due to a lab experiment gone awry when she was young. She wears a life-saving suit called the Ghost to regulate her matter density, but needs Pym's quantum technology to stay alive. (To add a mental level of trouble to Starr's predicament, it is actually Ava's parents' experiments that caused this damage as well as their own deaths, after her father, Elihas Starr, stole quantum technology from Pym.) They, as well as underground-market technology dealer Sonny Burch and his gang, take turns at trying to gain possession of the small-but-mighty lab, but after an action-packed series of chases, during which the lab changes hands several times, they ultimately fail to overcome the team of The Wasp, the X-Con Security Consultants, a super-sized Ant-Man, and the San Francisco Police Department.

95

Quantum Tunnel

Used by: Hank Pym, Hope Van Dyne, Scott Lang, Janet Van Dyne, Avengers
Years in use: The 1980s to the present day

Dr. Hank Pym and his scientist colleagues Bill Foster and Elihas Starr combine research efforts in the realm of quantum energy during their days together at S.H.I.E.L.D. One of the ambitious plans that Pym envisions in that era involves building a Quantum Tunnel, an elaborate structure that serves as a gateway to the quantum realm—the environment located at the subatomic level of existence. The relationship between Pym and Starr takes a turn for the worse after Starr attempts to steal Pym's tunnel plans, resulting in Pym firing and then discrediting Starr. During the rest of Pym's tenure at S.H.I.E.L.D., the Quantum Tunnel remains incomplete. He begins to develop his own Quantum Tunnel project after he launches Pym Tech, under which these blueprint plans are crafted.

In 1987, Pym's wife, Janet Van Dyne, was stranded in the Quantum Realm after she bravely used Pym Particles to shrink herself to subatomic size in order to disarm a Soviet missile. Years later, in 2015, Ant-Man Scott Lang is forced to shrink himself to subatomic size to defeat villainous Darren Cross' Yellowjacket and briefly enters the Quantum Realm before his suit's regulator pulls him back to normality. Before this occurs, however, Scott encounters Janet Van Dyne without knowing who she is.

When Pym learns of Scott's accidental yet successful trip to and from the Quantum Realm, he feels inspired to finish building his Quantum Tunnel. By doing so he hopes that he can finally bring his beloved Janet back to the macroscopic world and thereby salvage his relationship with their daughter Hope, who blames him for her mother's disappearance.

Three years later, Pym's tunnel plans come to fruition and he, Hope, and Scott achieve their goal of retrieving Janet Van Dyne from the Quantum Realm. At the same time their breakthrough invites undue attention from others with their own reasons for wishing to obtain Quantum Tunnel energy, including Starr's molecularly unstable daughter Ava, a.k.a. Ghost, and underground-market technology dealer Sonny Burch.

Pym, Janet, Hope, a.k.a. The Wasp, and Scott Lang build a more compact version of Pym's Quantum Tunnel, small enough to be housed in the back

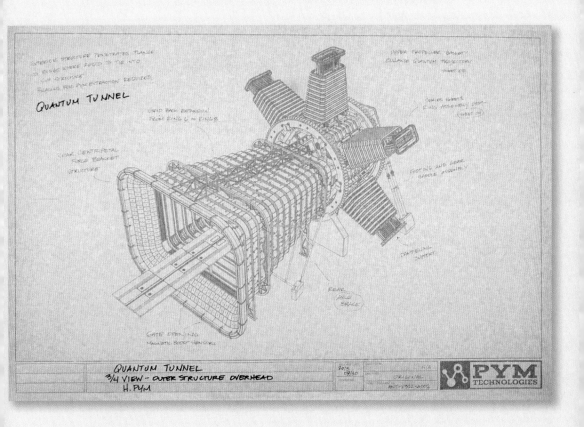

of a van. This tunnel works, and Scott retrieves healing particles to cure Ava Starr. Unfortunately the group's test run is badly timed, taking place just as Thanos causes the Snap, which removes the Pym-Van Dyne family from existence and leaves Scott stranded in the Quantum Realm.

Scott is pulled back into his full-size human existence five years later, when a rat, lurking in the long-stored van, happens to knock the tunnel controls back into action.

Once Scott gets his bearings and comes to realize the nature of the major incident that took place while he was adrift in the Quantum Realm, he seeks out his remaining Avengers allies and sparks an idea to use the Quantum Realm's power to initiate the Time Heist, so that Thanos' elimination of half of all life in the universe never takes place. After the Quantum Tunnel machine in Pym's van proves faulty, the Avengers seek to convince Tony Stark to come out of retirement to brainstorm a new

Pym's Quantum Tunnel—as built in his portable lab many years after his initial plans were drawn up.

After the Snap and at Scott Lang's suggestion, Tony Stark builds this version of a Quantum Tunnel.

quantum path forward. Stark's work with Rocket and a renewed alliance among the surviving Avengers leads to the construction of a Quantum Tunnel to use the Quantum Realm to travel to different points in time. These ultimately prevent Thanos from gathering all six Infinity Stones in the first place.

Some of those involved in this Quantum Realm mission pay the ultimate price: both Natasha Romanoff, a.k.a. Black Widow, and Tony Stark sacrifice their lives for the greater good. On the other hand, Steve Rogers finds peace in the time-travel opportunity the Quantum Tunnel provides, choosing to live out his remaining years in a timeline that places him together with his one true love, Peggy Carter.

96

Hand Surgery Rig

Created for: Dr. Stephen Strange
Year in use: 2016

This surgical construction reflects the work of an ambitious medical practitioner who is assigned a high stakes task: repairing the means of livelihood of a fellow doctor. That fellow doctor has a conflicting impression, convinced that this combination of pins and braces marks the end of his illustrious career.

The hands on which this design is based are those of Dr. Stephen Strange, a renowned neurosurgeon who is at the top of his game until an evening of distracted, aggressive driving in harsh weather conditions sends him plunging to the bottom of both his career and a steep cliff. He is pulled from the wreckage after the "golden hours" for nerve recovery expire, and when he awakens from surgery to see this structure fused onto his precious hands, he fears the worst.

Dr. Christine Palmer assures Strange that the surgeon has done his best under the circumstances, describing the 11-hour surgery in detail. This involved placing 11 stainless-steel pins in the bones and dealing with multiple torn ligaments and severe nerve damage in both hands. However, Strange is unable to see beyond his proud belief that he was the best man to do the job, if only he had had his own hands available to do it.

After the pins are removed, Strange deals with his predicament with minimal patience, frustrated by all traditional medical methods of recuperation, regardless of the expense and expertise involved. Strange's life and recovery soon take a very different path as he discovers Kamar Taj in Nepal, a training facility that guides him toward a physical, psychological, and mystical evolution beyond even his brilliant mind's wildest imaginings.

Files regarding Dr. Strange's hand repair surgeries, which required great expense and expertise to solve—way beyond traditional medical practices.

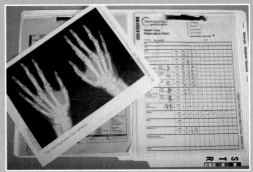

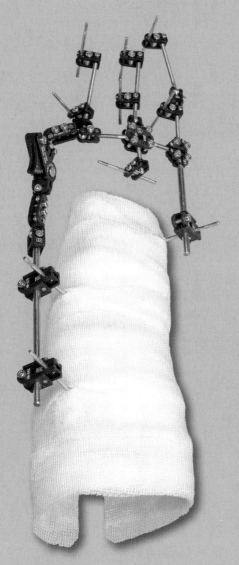

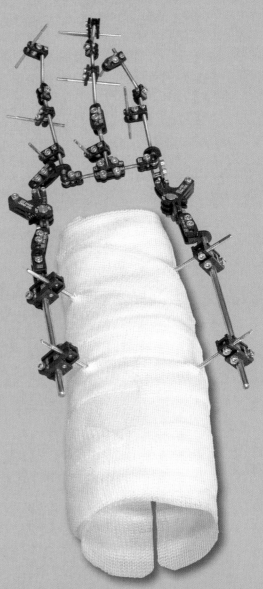

97

A Vial of Vibranium

Used by: Wakandan and Talokanil scientists, Howard Stark, Ultron
Years in use: Unknown to the present day

Vibranium is a powerful natural resource, the rarest metal on the planet, an element born of a meteorite that collided with Earth in ancient times. Fragments from the meteor's impact landed in a region of Africa and in the Atlantic Ocean adjacent to the Yucatan Peninsula. The humans that inhabit these regions—namely the Wakanda and Talokanil peoples—evolved and learned to work with the precious metal and apply it to many uses, including revolutionizing their societies' technology in virtually every major field: medical, weaponry, transportation, and communications.

Vibranium appears as an indigo ore in its purest form and often casts a similar purple radiance, observable as an aura emanating from energy powered by its essence and in plant life that has grown in vibranium-rich soils. A purple-flowered plant, the Heart-Shaped Herb, that has evolved under vibranium growing conditions is central to important Wakandan ceremonies. Any potential ruler must partake of the herb in order to commune with the ancestors before inheriting the great responsibility of becoming the Black Panther, protector of the Wakandan nation. (Vibranium also strengthens the Black Panther's suit, greatly increasing its ability to absorb kinetic energy.) The herb bolsters the Black Panther's speed, strength, agility, and intelligence, helping to ensure he or she will be a wise ruler, and an extract from it provides a life-saving medicine.

Early generations of the Talokanil evolved to be able to live and function in the depths of the Atlantic Ocean thanks to a drink made from a vibranium-infused flower. Like the Wakandans on land, the Talokanil have used vibranium to create a society filled with technological marvels, achievements far in advance of even the richest nations on Earth.

Because the Wakandan and Talokanil people understand the power and limited availability of vibranium, they conscientiously try to keep their resources closely protected, even to the point of masking their environments from the rest of humankind and also from extraterrestrial

species. Despite their security measures—which in Wakanda's case includes creating a shield over the country's high-tech capital that makes it look like that of an economically poor country—vibranium slowly finds its way into the wider world through various underground trafficking efforts, such as those pioneered by N'Jobu and Ulysses Klaue in the 1990s. This illegal trade ultimately enables terrifyingly anti-human artificial intelligence Ultron to use the mineral to create a doomsday weapon in 2015. Ultron also uses vibranium in the construction of a synthezoid whom he hopes to use to defeat the Avengers. However, Tony Stark uploads his own A.I., JARVIS into the body of the synthezoid, who turns against his murderous creator and helps the Avengers defeat him. The vibranium-bodied synthezoid subsequently joins the Avengers as Vision.

In the dark days of World War II, a small quantity of the element comes into the possession of top Strategic Scientific Reserve inventor Howard Stark. He soon puts this vibranium to good use, creating a prototype shield for the Army's one and only super soldier, Captain America.

Before long the shield is finished with an iconic coat of red-white-and-blue detail work and goes into service as a protective device and an awesome throwing weapon. One of vibranium's many remarkable qualities is its sheer durability. It never seems to tarnish, rust, or deteriorate. Cap's vibranium shield even withstands being submerged for decades in the freezing waters of the Arctic without showing any signs of age.

This ancient Wakandan ax has a vibranium head —as revealed with a wipe by Ulysses Klaue.

The original silver
vibranium shield Cap
spotted in Stark's lab
back in 1943.

98

Kimoyo Beads

Used by: Wakandan citizens
Years in use: Unknown to the present day

Kimoyo beads are a prime example of the ingenuity of Wakandan science and technology contained within a stylish yet super-functional object.

At first glance, one might assume Kimoyo beads are simply a decorative bracelet worn by Wakandan citizens. However, they are far more useful and technologically advanced than they appear. Developed and produced by the Wakandan Design Group, Kimoyo beads can be used as a means of communication, for spatial and transportation access, for information storage, and more, depending on the role of the Wakandan wearing them. The beads are made from vibranium, appear in varied combinations of black and metallic finishes, and exhibit a variety of symbols, reflecting what each bead controls or contains.

Beads may serve medical purposes, as shown by T'Challa's and Shuri's use of them to heal a bullet wound for C.I.A. Agent Everett Ross. Shuri's beads also give her the means to scan items such as Vision's Mind Stone implant before attempting to remove it with great care, to share imagery via holographic projection, and to control vehicles, even beyond the borders of Wakanda.

When Shuri is kidnapped by the Talokanil, her Kimoyo beads are found under pieces of wreckage by Ross. Queen Ramonda contacts him through them and Ross learns of Shuri's kidnap and the threat to global security of the emergence of a "new world power."

The beads that Okoye possesses have diverse capabilities, including allowing her to access the throne room and other elite facilities in the kingdom, to fly the Royal Talon Fighter, to project holograms, and to communicate with T'Challa. The beads also project a personal energy shield, and the means of navigation and surveillance services in the form of audio and video recordings from either a stationary position or a drone-like flying machine.

99

Vibranium Gauntlets

Used by: Shuri

Years in use: 2016 to the present day

Shuri holds important titles in Wakanda, including Princess and Black Panther, but one of her most significant roles is as leader of the Wakandan Design Group. Her genius as an inventor leads to numerous advances in science and technology.

The creation of these gauntlets is just one example of her skills. These weapons pay visual homage to the iconic panther of Wakandan culture but roar with true power, emitting powerful blasts of energy. Shuri dons them when she, Nakia, and Agent Ross step in to support T'Challa's effort to regain control of Wakanda from N'Jadaka and his forces. Within seconds of entering the fray, Shuri aims the gauntlets at two opponents and blasts them off of their feet with a burst of blue energy. She later turns the gauntlets on N'Jadaka at close range, but is challenged by another one of her creations in that combat—the vibranium Black Panther suit he wears absorbs the gauntlets' energy and then turns it back on her. At the same time, his vibranium spear makes contact and seemingly shorts out her right gauntlet.

Shuri does not abandon the gauntlets after their service against N'Jadaka, however. She later fires one of them at Corvus Glaive as he enters her laboratory seeking the Mind Stone from Vision during Thanos' quest to gather all six Infinity Stones. She also wields them in battle against Thanos in 2023, as part of the grand alliance from Earth and beyond that rallies to reverse the lethal Snap of five years prior in which Shuri herself had disappeared alongside half of all creation. Fortunately, Shuri's fighting spirit and fiery gauntlets are alive and well in this high-stakes moment of conflict, playing their part in the successful elimination of Thanos once and for all.

A top view of one of
Shuri's gauntlets.

100

Adam's Birthing Pod

Used by: Ayesha, Adam
Year in use: 2014

This golden chamber is what the Sovereign call a birthing pod, a cocoon-type space in which a creature is intentionally grown. This particular object is utilized by Ayesha, the High Priestess of the Sovereign, as a tool in her plot to seek revenge upon the Guardians of the Galaxy after they apparently renege on her contracted assignment to protect Anulax Batteries, a precious energy source.

Ayesha grows her own weapon to defeat the Guardians, and names him Adam. He is awakened from this Birthing Pod slightly earlier than expected so that the High Evolutionary, creator of the Sovereign, can achieve a compatible goal. The High Evolutionary desires to recapture his own creation—89P13—a genetically and bionically enhanced raccoon who, as Rocket, also happens to be part of the Guardians of the Galaxy.

Adam sets forth on his combined mission to capture 89P13 and kill the rest of the Guardians but faces multiple setbacks in his quest, including a knock-down, drag-out battle on Knowhere. Adam returns to the High Evolutionary's Arête Laboratories to be healed. After another round of warfare against the Guardians, Adam ultimately learns that the High Evolutionary means to inflict genocide upon those planets and creatures that fail to live up to his almost impossibly perfect criteria, including his own Sovereign kind. He has a change of heart after being saved by Groot in the midst of battle and witnessing the Guardians going to great lengths to save the innocent Star Children and animals from Counter-Earth.

Adam demonstrates his new allegiance by saving Star-Lord from death in the cold of outer space and then joining the ragtag team of universal protectors. Although the Birthing Pod was meant to hatch a being to bring an end to the Guardians, it turns out to be a source of next-generation growth for the team.

Index

SENIOR EDITOR Alastair Dougall
PROJECT ART EDITOR Chris Gould
DESIGNER Lisa Robb
PRODUCTION EDITOR Siu Yin Chan
SENIOR PRODUCTION CONTROLLER Laura Andrews
MANAGING EDITOR Rachel Lawrence
MANAGING ART EDITOR Vicky Short
MANAGING DIRECTOR Mark Searle

First published in Great Britain in 2024 by
Dorling Kindersley Limited
One Embassy Gardens, 8 Viaduct Gardens,
London SW11 7BW
A Penguin Random House Company
10 9 8 7 6 5 4 3 2 1

001–342640–Oct/2024
Page design copyright © 2024 Dorling Kindersley Limited

© 2024 MARVEL

The authorised representative in the EEA is Dorling Kindersley
Verlag GmbH. Arnulfstr. 124, 80636 Munich, Germany.

All rights reserved. Without limiting the rights under the
copyright reserved above, no part of this publication may be
reproduced, stored in, or introduced into a retrieval system,
or transmitted, in any form, or by any means (electronic,
mechanical, photocopying, recording, or otherwise), without
the prior written permission of the copyright owner.

A CIP catalogue record for this book
is available from the British Library.
ISBN 978-0-2416-9191-5

Printed and bound in China
www.dk.com
www.marvel.com

ACKNOWLEDGMENTS

DK Publishing would like to thank Kevin Feige, Louis D'Esposito,
Brad Winderbaum, Jacqueline Ryan-Rudolph, Capri Ciulla,
Nigel Goodwin, Erika Denton, Jennifer Wojnar, Jeff Willis,
Jennifer Giandalone, Vince Garcia, Sarah Truly Beers, and
Kristy Amornkul at Marvel Studios; Sarah Singer and
Jeff Youngquist at Marvel; and Chelsea Alon, John Morgan III,
and Shana C. Highfield at Disney Publishing Worldwide.
DK would also like to thank Julia March
for proofreading and for the index.

PICTURE CREDITS

Necrosword pp. 98–9: Tim Flattery
The Darkhold p. 104: Ivan Weightman
Widow's Bite p. 177: Fabian Lacey

MIX
Paper | Supporting
responsible forestry
FSC™ C018179

This book was made with Forest
Stewardship Council™ certified
paper – one small step in DK's
commitment to a sustainable future.
Learn more at www.dk.com/uk/
information/sustainability

ABOUT THE AUTHOR

Tracey Miller-Zarneke first became fascinated by the MCU
through the eyes of her sons. She then became fully educated
through the blessing of forced pandemic "quarantime"
and access to Disney+. Tracey continues to enjoy being
a student and fan of all things Marvel in between writing books,
publicity materials and strategic communications.
Tracey is also co-author of DK's *The Disney Book* (2023).

AUTHOR'S ACKNOWLEDGMENTS

The author wishes to thank her amazing DK partners; the
ever-patient and diligent Alastair Dougall for his editorial
prowess; Chris Gould and the ultra-talented Lisa Robb for her
continued graphic design partnership in our project pairings.
This book would not be possible without the help and fact-
checking of John Morgan III, Chelsea Alon, Jackie Ryan,
and Sarah Singer, thus the author sends much appreciation their
way. And as always, the author is grateful for the support of her
family co-existing with her countless hours at her desk and
screens, virtually exploring every corner of the MCU in the
making of this book—she says to the Zarneke clan, know that
"I love you 3000."